Say "Yes" To Love

God's Guidance to LightWorkers

Through Yaël and Doug Powell

Say 'Yes' To Love,
God's Guidance to LightWorkers
Through Yaël and Doug Powell.

Cover illustration and book layout by Judith Bicking
Compilation, editing of Messages by Shanna Mac Lean

Websites: www.circleoflight.net
www.sayyestolove.net
Email: sayyes@circleoflight.net

Printing: InstantPublisher.com Collierville,TN

WHAT IS A LightWorker?

A LightWorker is anyone on Earth who is truly committed in his or her heart to helping others awaken to Love. Light is the pathway by which Love enters. Our hearts open with Love. Love makes life "lighter." We shed light on difficult situations with Love.

LightWorkers can be explorers in the metaphysical realms. They have expansive vision. They do not accept the world as a place of inevitable discord, war and hardship. They are people who have asked questions and they have not accepted easy or conventional answers. They know the power of our thought and they know the power of Love.

LightWorkers are everywhere – in every religion, in every walk of life. Many of them would not describe themselves in any special way. Love knows no boundaries, no definitions.

Say "Yes" To Love Series
through Yaël and Doug Powell

In Publication

Say "Yes" to Love, God Explains SoulMates

Say "Yes" to Love, God Unveils SoulMate Love
and Sacred Sexuality

Say "Yes" to Love, God's Guidance to LightWorkers

In Preparation, soon to be published

Say "Yes" to Love, God Leads Humanity
Toward Christ Consciousness

Words From Our Readers

"I proceed very slowly reading these Messages because it's as if it weren't my eyes that were reading it, but my heart. It's as if I've just come Home. Your Messages are so "soft." I don't know how else to describe them. It feels like being wrapped in something very delicate. I keep crying all the time when I read them… I feel so very beloved."
Paula Launonen, Ravenna, Italy

"Reading the Messages from God is like communing with God. Even if they are addressed to all humanity, they can also be a very personal experience. When you read the Messages from God, your heart will open and stay open if you so choose. A cascade of sparkling, fresh, flowing, colored Love energy. In Love from Love to Love creating more Love. I will be thankful forever."
Tiziana Paggiolu, London, England

"Everything in the Messages resonates so deeply in me. I am amazed that I've found so much in the Messages that had already been revealed to me in visions and dreams…it sometimes takes my breath away! It has given so much validity to everything I had already come to believe. Thank you all for feeling the need to share the Messages. They have meant so much to me in my journey. It's kind of like piloting a boat by the stars and one day discovering a secret compartment full of maps that show where all the ports of call are located. It makes it so much easier to get where you want to go!"
Diane Dunville, Lanexa, VA

"I am so grateful for the dedication and hard work that has granted us these tools for our speed-breaking evolution. These divinely gifted Messages explain the real difference between having sex and making love. What the world needs NOW is love, sweet love."
Tracy Bowdle, Rogers, AR

"These Messages are stunning, clear, beautiful, re-activating, stirring to the core of my being. This material reminds me of Home, reminds me to express the totality of my being, reminds me of how close to Home we are now, reminds me of my Twin Flame. Just having the books and knowing their content is a small sign of the ecstasy to come."

Karen Porrit, U.K.

"These Messages, faithfully documented by Yaël Powell, were brought to me at just the right time in my life and served as validation of what my Twin Flame and I had discovered on our own, without any outside influence. I can speak personally on the validity of this Twin Flame relationship as I was blessed enough in my lifetime to have been with my Twin Flame. Our story is for another time and another place, but it is important to state without qualification that the reality of the soulmate bond as expressed through God's Messages is not a fabrication or an idealistic view of what love can be... It is the greatest love that can be, the love of our Creator to us, and the ability to experience that kind of love within our soulmate bond."

Rev. Adelle Tilton, The Church of Interfaith Christians, NE

"I have thoroughly enjoyed reading the Messages from God. As you read you feel a personal connection with God and feel as though you are being spoken to personally. You are lovingly and joyously led to remember that through love all we need will be fulfilled. Thank you so much for sharing these messages with us. Love and hugs.

Janet Krager, La Salle, IL

"Reading these messages has altered my way of thinking about life, soulmates and myself. I no longer see myself as the small body that I have come to think I was. I know that I am part of God. Also, even though most of the time I still feel alone, every day, more and more I realize that I am not alone, that I have a soulmate who is with me all the time. As I read the Messages from God I feel more at peace within myself and I am comforted. I am so glad that I have found these Messages and they have altered my life for the better."

Lori Goodman, San Diego, CA

DEDICATION

We dedicate this book to God,
who is the All of Love we serve with every
breath in every moment and in all we are
together. We are so deeply grateful for the
amazing ways that God grows us, step by
careful step, with such tender and personal
Love. May we truly be in God's Will
completely as we serve Love's great
awakening.

We also dedicate this book to the
beautiful Lightworkers who are our soul
family, the ever-expanding Circle of Light
team around the world. And to all
LightWorkers, our sisters and brothers
everywhere, we dedicate these Messages
and extend our Love and deepest thanks
for your work. May the breathtaking years
before us be all we know they are meant
to be, as Love becomes the truth of life for
humanity and Earth.

In Memoriam

In memory of my beautiful son, Joshua Michael,
the greatest being of light I have known on Earth.
It has taken twenty-five years to mend the hole in my trust
in God that his death produced. However, this mending
opened an even greater communion and a deeper Love with
God, and brought forth these Messages.

I know that I will see Joshua Michael again, as the veil comes
down and the illusion of death fades away. How I will rejoice
to be in his radiant presence once again!

SAY 'YES' TO LOVE
God's Guidance to LightWorkers

TABLE OF CONTENTS

ACKNOWLEDGEMENTS

I first acknowledge my beloved Doug, my SoulMate, whom I love more deeply every day. Doug's increasing light and clarity is a continual inspiration to me and to all who know him. We have truly walked every step of this path together, from being two individuals full of fear and ego, to recognizing our SoulMate relationship and claiming daily more of the passion, beauty and ecstasy that God keeps lovingly showing us. I am so deeply grateful to God for tenderly unveiling to me my magnificent SoulMate, Doug.

I am also grateful for Doug's amazing perspective, and his ability to bring the vision and light of these Messages into grounded action in daily life. We are the perfect balance. I am the visionary, the mystic, lifted by God to the shores of the New World. Doug is the bridge, the capable hands and compassionate heart that grounds and makes accessible to all of us on Earth this vision we serve to bring forth.

Next I acknowledge Shanna, soul sister and great light, who loves God as much as I do. To share such passionate dedication to God and to share it on a daily basis is a wonder. Only God could have orchestrated the miracle of Shanna in our lives! Not only is she spiritual family, she is also completely dedicated to living beyond ego, in the heart. Only this commitment in all of us could have produced the amazing harmony and joy of our co-creative efforts. It is Shanna's dynamic energy, dedication and skills that have brought these Messages forth, both in book form and on the Internet. Shanna is a LightWorker in every atom of her being. I am honored to know and love her.

I acknowledge my beautiful soul sister, Michelle, whose glorious voice and loving heart are also dedicated to bringing forth the vision of what this world is meant to be. The music of the spheres is her inspiration. The star-studded sky is her cathedral. She embodies all that is pure and perfect on the Earth. I am honored to share this path of service with her, and forever to be her friend.

I thank our sweet Mary, whose life belongs totally to God, for typing these Messages and blessing them with her Love. May she ever be a part of our team, being grown and nourished as we are by these Messages. I acknowledge her husband, Steve, and her son, Michael, a young man who was raised completely conscious of spiritual reality. He is amazing!

I deeply thank Suzanne Mueller, the woman who saved my life by taking me out of the absolute terror of a life filled with sexual and physical abuse and horrible darkness. Suzanne placed my feet upon the Path of Light by teaching me to meditate thirty years ago, thus establishing in my life the spiritual practice that has ultimately brought forth these Messages.

I acknowledge Bernadine Greer, the most generous and most beautiful light I have ever known. Bernadine was in my life in the early years when I was coping with such disability that I could barely move. She would bathe me in Love and most especially, give me hope. Bernadine is no longer on the physical plane. It is with glad heart that I picture her watching over me.

To everyone who has touched my life, I give thanks!

Yaël

I am excited about this book because it is a helpful guide on how to live one's life. We all need friends, teachers and guides to assist us when we are lost or confused. So I would like to acknowledge my friends far and wide.

Most especially I would like to acknowledge my SoulMate, Yaël, who has helped me to grow immensely over the last sixteen years, and who, through her Love and dedication to God, continues to bring forth these remarkable Messages. Thank you.

Doug

INTRODUCTION

The world is filled with light, with messages of awakening pouring through everywhere and LightWorkers shining forth in every country the world over. For those of us who came here to assist the transformation, it is an experience like nothing else in our lives. Tears wash our cheeks, gratitude fills our hearts as what we have always known in our hearts becomes manifest in the world. No matter what we have been told, deep inside we knew that Love was the only truth, that life is meant to be filled with joy. We have known there was another way than that which this world has called life.

Such has been my experience with these Messages. When I sit to meditate I am lifted, illumined, washed in God's presence. I am filled with such Love that there are no human words for it. And as much as I can hold of God's truth and God's glorious light, I am given. Sometimes whole "packets" of information are gently dropped into my consciousness. Other times I am given the actual experience of how we are meant to live. Yet with every one of these, there is one overarching feeling – God reaching for humanity, passionately with tenderness and yearning. Each time I give my Will to God and I become the pen in God's hand, bringing through that Love that it can touch us here, as we live these lives on Earth.

Although I always remember the experience, I rarely remember the words. It is an experience of heart and light for me and not the mind. So each day when we read the Message given, I am hearing it for the first time in words. Often the tears come as I recognize how perfectly God is leading us, opening us, bring us Home to Love. And oh, the tears of gratitude when we receive the reassurance that we WILL bring all of our beloved humanity with us, that the truths inside us will become the reality in which we live.

As you open this book, you open to a journey of magnificence, for starting here and going on through two more books (and counting) God will bring you with personal care, gently to Christ Consciousness – to the place where we know who we are with such conviction that nothing can dissuade us – across the Divide, into the New World.

Please read with your heart! Let go of the judgments of your mind. Allow the light beneath the words to come through to you and allow it to bring you the experience of God's presence.

Each of us has a different "piece" that we are bringing through. Ours are these Messages that began almost 30 years ago, blossoming into outgoing Messages in earnest when Doug and I came together in 1986.

Like many LightWorkers, I entered this life bringing light into great darkness. I knew the deep betrayal of incest, and the anguish of both physical and emotional abuse. My father was the instrument of abuse and darkness that spanned my entire life until I was 21. That year my father died, and all of the energies surrounding him turned their full attention to me, bringing with them an experience of abject terror.

In desperation I searched for help and answers.

Knowing nowhere else to turn and believing my father was seeking entry to the physical world again through me, I went to a spiritualist church. There I met the minister, Suzanne Mueller, who changed my life forever.

Suzanne explained to me that rather than explore what was happening, I needed to raise my vibration until such energies could not touch me. She explained that I could do this through meditation. I began right away. Five years of terror later, I succeeded in closing my connection to the astral world, which my father had carefully opened. Looking back I could even be grateful because I could see that he had assisted me to develop my abilities to communicate telepathically and to experience things beyond our normal world. So it was that I discovered my deep dedication to the light, through the darkness of abuse and terror into the glorious light of God. From the moment Suzanne taught me to meditate, I have steadfastly and resolutely set aside at least an hour each and every day to meditate, no matter what was happening in my life.

I studied with Suzanne for seven years, learning about the Masters, and studying every spiritual path. Suzanne continued to grow me in my abilities to reach into an expanded universe and to receive and experience information. I received guidance from God regularly. Eventually I also began to channel for Suzanne, but as time went on, I slowly realized that something was not right with the channeling. In a way I could not explain, the energy had switched. I grasped that we were being manipulated by the beings supposedly assisting us to serve the light.

This was a deeply traumatic experience for me and brought about the only time I have ever stopped meditating for any reason. I threw away all my crystals, returned to my Arkansas cabin in the woods and clearly made the decision that from that moment the only energy that I would ever allow to come through me was God. I had never spoken anything with such passion or conviction, nor had I ever meant anything so much. Right away I felt the connection with God restored, each day sitting in light in God's presence. I was aware of God clearly leading me, but I was not yet able to translate this into words.

In 1983, I was diagnosed with a genetic disease of the spine (from which my father had also suffered). I could no longer work. I had to leave school to which I had returned to further my education. I was in excruciating pain and could barely get out of bed. I decided I did not want to continue to live in such a state. I began to make plans for suicide. I ordered books from the Hemlock Society. I collected drugs.

Then, in meditation, God came to me. I was lifted and blessed. I was washed in light. But most importantly, I knew God's Love as a personal experience. My life has never been the same. I knew I needed to live. I knew that I had to decide again, as I had a number of times before, to stay on Earth, even though it didn't feel like home to me. I began to record God's Messages to me, Messages that gave me courage to live each day in pain. These Messages spoke of reasons for the things I experience, and truly they saved my life.

In 1986 I met Doug. I had dreamed of him before we met. I knew he was my destiny. In December we married and sitting together in meditation for the first time, God revealed that destiny. As I closed my eyes and touched Doug's hand, my entire being exploded into light. God's loving presence grew. Light shone around us both and we were alive in luminous golden light. We each seemed to be a flame, lit from within by God. The flame burst forth, jumped the gap between us and poured forth from us in an outgoing river of Love reaching for humanity. We were to serve together.

In the midst of this experience I found a notebook and pen and I wrote. As I wrote I was aware of being assisted with the energy, but I was also aware that, though illuminated by God's Love, I was doing my best with my words to describe that which is indescribable.

Thus these Messages began. They have now lovingly, unfailingly guided us through fifteen years of marriage. They have kept us going when we were ready to give up. They have explained ourselves to us. They have revealed to us our destiny. And as we have grown together as a result of God's tender guiding love, we have also grown in our ability to raise ourselves up to meet God at a higher level. In doing so, we have been greatly blessed with the understanding of the "piece" of information that it is our destiny to share.

We had prayed that our next step for the Messages be revealed, along with the resources and people to bring it forth. In July of 2001 God brought us the joy of uniting with a key member of our soul family, Shanna. When Shanna took up permanent residence at Circle of Light in December, we all experienced a great shift in consciousness, a transformation for all of us.

In a series of Messages that became our first two books, God explained the significance of SoulMates, Sacred Sexuality and God's amazing gift to us. Unlike the unfolding of normal spiritual law, we now have a special dispensation from God. SoulMates will now come together before we are living perfect Love. The SoulMates will bring Love to Earth, opening the hearts of humankind.

God has led us absolutely impeccably through a light-filled awakening of a greater and greater spiritual communion. Fear has fallen away, as God carefully showed us how to move beyond ego and how to fill our days with gratitude. In a very short span of time, the Messages contained in this book poured forth. Even in all of my sweet and glorious communion with God, I had never experienced anything like this. I was lifted in vibrating waves of golden light.

Each day we would read and absorb the Message. Some of the Messages were answers to our questions, questions that arose as we took in and lived what God had given. Other Messages were poured through me like a rushing river headed outward to humanity. In many of the Messages there is repetition. Yet this repetition is both necessary and purposeful. Every time God repeats something, it is because this is what it takes to make it into our consciousness. You will also find in reading, that every repetition brings with it another new piece, one that requires the repeated concept as its foundation. Another thing to notice is the level at which you read. If you are only in your mind, the repetition may catch your attention. But if you are prayerful, with an open heart, you will be lifted perfectly, step-by-step, concept-by-concept until the shift is born within you.

We offer these Messages with the deepest gratitude and humility and with the continual prayer that we may be only in God's Will, that we may be completely clear and free of self in our receipt and offering of these Messages.

The Messages have completely changed our lives. Even the Messages we could not immediately understand nonetheless blessed us and moved us into greater awareness.

We pray for you these same miracles, for as the coming of Love for this age takes shape in your life, it will completely change your definitions of life and of Love. Then will you too show this path to others.

A Note From the Editor

I met Yaël and Doug Powell on July 17th, 2001. God led me right to them through a series of synchronous events. Because of her disability, Yaël rarely leaves her home but she and Doug had decided very spontaneously to celebrate her birthday at the home of a close friend in Fayetteville. That friend had also graciously agreed to host me, a complete stranger, for a few days, while I explored the Fayetteville, AR area.

As I sat with Yaël and Doug that evening, I was fascinated by their obvious living Love for each other, a Love that pervaded their every word and movement. I learned about Yaël's constant pain from a genetic disease of the spine that severely limits her movement, and about Circle of Light, their spiritual center in Eureka Springs. Following dinner Yaël read one of the "Messages from God" that have come through her during thirty years of daily meditation. I felt indescribable excitement and upliftment from the extraordinary vibration created and the amazing information of this Message.

We quickly recognized ourselves as the ancient soul family we are, and spent two bliss filled days together at Circle of Light, reconnecting, sharing our lives and our spiritual journeys. Our coming together was divinely guided, step-by-step. Yaël and Doug showed me fifty hand-written notebooks of Messages from God! I committed myself on the spot to utilizing my writing, editing and organizational skills to help them bring this illuminated and needed material out into the world. I returned to my home in Black Mountain, N.C., tidied up my life and made plans for a move. Our first joint publication effort, *Say "Yes" to Love, God Explains SoulMates*, was accomplished from a distance, and just before Christmas 2001 I took up residence in my new home at Circle of Light Spiritual Center.

After my arrival our "training" began in earnest. The daily Messages intensified, many with specific personal directives for each of us. We all experienced a series of great shifts in consciousness that are ongoing. Within a few months we had the entire content of two more books in the **Say "Yes" to Love** series, **God Unveils SoulMate Love and Sacred Sexuality**, as well as the present book, **God's Guidance to LightWorkers**. Recently the Messages and our inner training has been directed to what God is calling "approaching and accepting Christ Consciousness." As quickly as we absorb what is being taught and how we are being grown, the material is edited to be outgoing to humanity. With humility and honor, we accept our roles as conduits. Thus, the fourth book in the **Say "Yes" series, God Leads Humanity Toward Christ Consciousness** will soon be published.

Life at Circle of Light is a series of miracles. The natural beauty of the lake, mountains and surrounding woods creates a vibration of the New World. The evening sunsets are otherworldly. We watch in awe. Every day Yaël meditates several hours, bringing through the amazing teachings from God. The highlight of each day is reading the new Message together. I assist in managing our active wedding business, spend a great deal of time in sorting, compiling and editing Messages, direct the growing communication from our website, www.circleoflight.net, help with cooking and practical life necessities and tend the organic garden. I have the joyous feeling of knowing I am in the right place at the right time, with my soul family, doing the tasks for which I have long been prepared. I have never been happier! Our commitment as a spiritual family is to bring God's Message of Love forth to our brothers and sisters.

Shanna Mac Lean

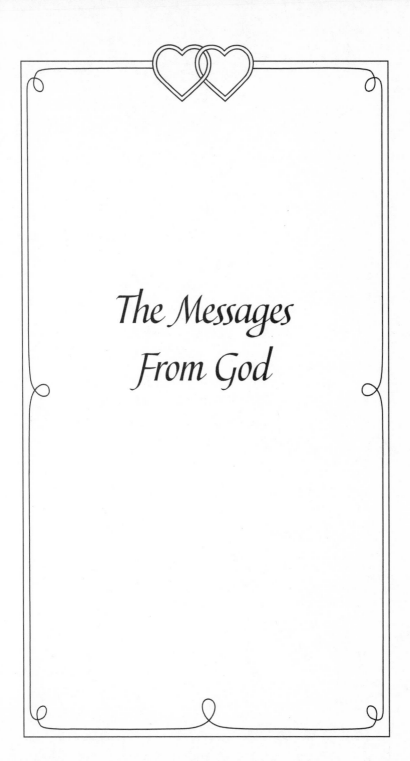

The Messages
From God

You have now entered
the Age of the Awakening Heart.
That is YOU, dear ones.
These next years will be aflame.
Oh, first a spark,
but then a fire,
and then a flame of Love
that will consume the Earth
and make of you new beings.
Is this not the real truth of **Revelation***?*
Oh, yes, the Earth will be consumed in flames,
dear ones – the flames of Love,
of growing passion, of excitement for life
– flames of your true nature.

Transformation:
The LightWorkers' Decision

August 7, 2001

*E*very being of light in all the heavens, every being of Love in all the worlds, every wash of starlight that is embodied, every planet pregnant with life—all are holding their breath. All are holding their breath as I call you to step forth completely out of your reality and to trust that the New World will be there to place your foot upon. As I breathe in My In-breath, I feel you as the greatest Love stirring within. I too am pregnant with anticipation. In all of the worlds, all of the expanding universes, all of the trillions of beings spreading their wings of truth, there is none like you.

Now the time comes for the greatest leap of faith, faith that says that what is in your heart is the real truth, while all the structure by which you have lived your lives is an illusion. You understand this certainly, but do you understand it enough to bet your life upon it? Do you understand it enough to step forth and trust that My Love will be there? And are you ready to do this in ways both great and small, without any comparison between the world you are leaving and the world on which you arrive?

Are you willing to give up your "human home"— the ideas you have had about what it means to be a human being? Can you start with a clean slate upon which I write the truth of your life, and then you live it, moment-by-moment, step-by-step, vision-by-vision, dream-by-dream?

Dear ones, there are three very important things that have happened which have already changed your world forever. You need to understand these things deeply as you take My hand and step away from the ledge of the known world, as you step into the knowledge of your place in My heart and the truth of the "world to come." Love is "switched on" when you become a functioning cell in My heart, the heart of God, awakening.

First, in 1987, at the time of the Harmonic Convergence of energies, you made a decision in the temple of your hearts. Until that moment, there was to be a splitting of the path. Those who could make the choice for Love were to move ever higher into the light to bring forth the manifestation of humanity's evolution. The others who did not say "yes," were going to gently "drop-down" into a slower evolution, there to continue to evolve, living with those of like vibration.

At that time I felt a tugging on My heart, dear ones —a longing for those who were to be left behind. I felt keenly the emptiness within as I acknowledged that some cells of My heart would be missing, so to speak, still cloaked in illusion and darkness. You must understand that you do live within Me, and that you truly are living cells that are within My heart.

As this intense longing deepened, it became almost agonizing. Yes, I can feel agony and often have at the loss of communion with My own heart that the illusion has caused. When I looked within, I discovered something truly amazing! The longing that I was feeling was you, My LightWorkers, longing for your brothers and sisters. You did not want to leave them behind. You were My heart speaking to Me!

When I understood this, oh, My beautiful children, I

fell in Love with you all over again. I understood My own heart in new ways. I knew for the first time that you truly were showing Myself to Me. You were truly opening into Love in manifestation. I knew then that all I had dreamed of for you would be true. You would be co-creators gently loving new life into being—both within you and around you. I knew that your Homecoming was going to be more than all I had dreamed. I knew that in spite of the depth of illusion into which you had fallen, you were going to emerge as something more beautiful than either of us had ever dreamed.

So, there at that moment, that juncture when so much was held in the balance, you decided together, in unison, in your hearts, on the deepest spiritual plane that you can access, that you would offer yourselves, your service and your light so that nobody would be left behind! This was the moment of My greatest joy, for you are the wild card within Me. You are the part of Me that is unknown. You surprised Me in wondrous and wonderful ways.

At that moment all beings of light who assist you, concurred. It was and is possible for the children of God, using both your Love and your Will, to lift up and clean up everything in the world, so that nothing is left behind. *In order to do this, each of you agreed that you would personally transform the darkness, limitation and illusion for those who were not able or ready to do so.* You will gladly, you told Me, offer your Love and your service for the upliftment of the whole world, of humanity and the planet into the light.

Now we are here. We are on the very real cusp of the very real awakening. LightWorkers are remembering by the thousands daily that there are real and exciting changes. But many of you are not yet remembering your agreement of

3

service to the transformation.

The second thing that is happening, now that the changes are fully underway, is that many LightWorkers are finding themselves in unexpected situations of varying degrees of intensity— in the midst of difficult things for which there are no clear explanations. Beings of obvious light and very great Love are dealing with physical illnesses that even threaten to take them off the planet. Other beings are finding themselves in "financial crunch" though they know that I will always provide. The list goes on and on.

Many explanations are offered. These situations create fear and discomfort in those who are not so challenged. (If such a person as this who lives purely can be stricken, could this happen to me?). The ego rushes in and finds an excellent crack in the vibrations of Love, and judgment occurs. People are regularly told that they have done something to bring this on, or that they have not done their spiritual work. If all else fails, they are told that there must be some old subconscious pattern at work!

Dear ones, it is very important that you hear Me and this message of transformation. *We are now at the critical time.* One foot is on the shore of the New World and the other foot is on the shore of the Old. *Only the commitment of the LightWorkers, the pure and loving of heart, to use their lives, their bodies, hearts and Will in service to humanity's transformation will create the bridge that will bring everyone through.* To bring everyone was your promise to me. To bring everyone. Oh dear ones, this promise is how I know you are My children. All I am and more. This promise is how I know that Love will continue to show a new and more beautiful face, and that My heart will be a reflector of the pure light into the most glorious expression of our co-creation.

You must come to understand this process of transformation and this agreement. It has now become critical. If you do not, it could destroy the unity necessary to make the rise in consciousness and heart that will bring you back to The One. If you do not understand, then it will seem like chaos. It will seem that the laws of Love do not work. It will seem that the path of Love works for one person, opening them easily to obvious blessings and higher good, and does not work for another who is still suffering.

But the suffering is not their own, I tell you, My beloveds. *With the release from Time (and what you call Karma), with the extraordinary elevation in the light taking place, and with all the beings of light gathering here with you, any LightWorker choosing Love would be effortlessly rising, and everything of any negativity falling away. If that is not happening, then I guarantee you— that one is taking on the work of transformation for the rest of humanity.* This must be understood. It must be honored. It must be supported and assisted.

I ask this of all of you. In big ways or small, it is this tremendous service of doing more than your share that will bring all My children Home to Me now. And yes, ultimately all would return, but it is this extra effort that reveals your truth, your depth of Love and caring. Ultimately that will be reflected back to you in millions of ways. This too is a law of the universe, as you know.

So in this world of illusion it will be more important than ever to look very carefully at the truth of what is happening. Every situation must be read with the heart. Those who are living transformers will be obvious the moment you understand the fact of this most glorious offering.

Now, let Me remind you that this agreement that all humanity would make it Home in this evolution was a

. concord of all of you who have light enough to understand. If you are reading this, this means you. *So I must ask you to turn right now to Me and to ask Me to show you your path of service to this transformation.* You will be amazed. You'll find things making sense that just did not make sense to you. You'll understand the "piece," as you say, about giving that is the most powerful way to your own awakening. Of course, the Love that you give holds the most powerful blessing for you of all the energy you'll receive.

Dear ones, I will guide you. Here is the third and most important thing. This fact of the LightWorkers' offering of transformation will save the Earth and allow her to rise into her own process of ascension. All of you know this is her "initiation" also, yet you have not known how to assist her. As I have told you, energy must be dealt with. The "trash" must be cleaned up. This process of transformation when combined with your conscious intent is the most powerful energy available in this universe.

Now this seems like a big thing for Me to say, until you remember who I Am and thus who you are, co-creators who are the cells of My very heart. So all beings of light everywhere are on call to your intent. I want you to absorb this. Knowing this you must now take in the fact that *nothing that is happening here is personal. If you are a being of light, conscious of Me and dedicated to Love, the forces and powers that are working in your life are universal*—dramatic rivers of light, shifts in awareness of such magnitude that you cannot yet comprehend.

So you must not "put your head in the sand!" You must not believe that this is only about you, your growth, your awakening, your ascension. THAT VISION IS FAR TOO SMALL FOR YOU. If you subscribe to such a vision, you may keep your life progressing on a steady path upward but *you would be missing out on the most amazing, dramatic and beautiful Creation story ever lived: your Creation story!* It is the story where you, My children, activate your Will, light up the cells in My heart with such power and grace that you rectify a whole evolution by redeeming what had been forced into separation and illusion —all by the power of your choice, your Love and your Will.

Dear ones, you have often heard that for this time the coming of Christ will be within you. This process of taking on transformation for the world is exactly how you will do this. Christ on the cross did exactly the same thing. He saw that humanity had fallen prey to the illusion and He transformed it by living that darkness while in the body.

It is imperative that this information be distributed and understood. If you do not know what is happening as you take on the part of the transformation you have agreed to; if you run it through your body without the understanding and the intent of the transformative light, it can be too much for the physical vehicle. We do not want the experience of your piece of the transformation to be harmful in any way. But it can be because the energies are shifting, uplifting so rapidly that you must understand transformation. You must understand it because you have agreed to do it. On some level, in some way, your piece will come to you.

The worst thing that could happen is for you or others around you to place negativity upon the experience by seeing it as something wrong with you, your clarity, your clearing, your resolution of issues, your growth in Me. Every one of those thoughts creates a negative situation where there never was one. In other words although something negative is seeming to occur, in truth it is very positive, for your intention and the intention behind the whole situation is of the most profound good. Yet one judgment from yourself or others and the purity of the offering of this service is tainted, because you are co-creators and that thought creates a very real detrimental energy.

So please, dear ones, be so very careful. Be vigilant against judgment and negative interpretation. Be especially vigilant against the assumptions and easy answers that allow you to feel better than or separate from anyone. Those are the signs that the greatest offering of humanity thus far, the assurance of their divinity by this gift reflecting My fullness in each of you, has been commandeered by the ego or the intent of separation.

When you put your foot down on the shore of the New World, what you'll find instantly is a world totally in communion and communication, first through the Internet and then through the inner knowing. *You will find a world with a unity of purpose fully engaged in the process of transformation for all—not for the individual.* This, dear ones, is the difference between the Old World and the New World.

My Light Workers,
remember that each of you
is an "energy sorter."
As My light comes in, it is drawn first
to those with the vibrations
that match this light most closely.
This means that you of high vibration
have the opportunity
to qualify everything that comes in.
Please listen, dear ones.
This means that,
can you sustain the vibration,
you can "place" every bit of energy
coming to humanity.
You can send it forth to heal and bless
every single human being,
as well as Nature
and our beloved world.

Choosing Love.
The Truth of Good and Evil
and the Power of Our Attention

I am here, manifesting Love to you, in you and around you in all things. It is true that all things are Love. Creation is Love because Love is what I am. You understand that All That Is lives within Me, and some of you are beginning to glimpse that All That Is also lives within you. Now the question I hear from you is about good and evil and how to protect yourself from fear. Listen. ***The only protection from fear is the truth of Love.***

How shall we explain in words? In essence, it is something like this. Each SoulMate couple is a living cell in My heart. My heart is the generator of Love for All That Is, for all that lives in My body, mind and spirit. Thus, it is you, the SoulMates, through whom all My Love flows. All My Love, dear ones. This does not mean just the Love that flows into this world, for this world is one little daydream in your own vast consciousness (although one with a powerful connection to reality at the moment).

So, if you are one cell, then you are a portal of Love of a certain diameter. A certain amount of Love can and should pour through you at every moment as I interact as My Creation in such great and powerful Love. Now pay attention here. ***If you are fully present, if you accept who you are and take on your role as a cell of My heart, Love pours through you.*** It blazes through you and it blesses through you. Together with your SoulMate, you are the source for Love to move from My heart into Creation. If you are saying "yes"to Me, the portal is full of Love. It is wide open and full of Love. Nothing else can come through, right?

However, if you do not keep the full measure of your being open wide with Love, that means there is an area of the cell, your part of My heart, that has no energy. There is nothing moving through that area. *Dear ones, where Love is not, there is anti-Love. If Love for whatever reason abdicates, then there is no middle ground.* Thus, as the consciousness within the cells of My heart, if you do not take on your responsibility, you automatically create an opening for anti-Love to use.

Now, (keep stretching) when you are very close to Me, when your consciousness is bathed in Mine, you really cannot leave a part of your being blank, or untended, because you recognize yourself. You can't help it, because I always and continually show your true self to you. How could I not? I look at you. I turn My attention and I recognize you, My heart, My children. Since I am Love, you are the pieces of Me that will take forth what I am genetically, just as your human children do for you.

So when we are close, you can't help but remember who you are and you are open wide and Love is pouring through you continually. All is as it is meant to be, with My heart (you) delivering My Love to all Creation every moment. This keeps all Creation filled up with Love and at the same time prevents the existence of any other energy.

However, if you move away from Me, you are ever more vulnerable to losing My assurance to you of who you are. This was not meant to happen. It was always My intention to experience the glorious expansion of My heart into every fascinating possibility while fully connected, with

12

the cells of My heart fully aware of who they are and thus containing only Love.

Yet, to allow you to fully become My co-creators, independent in consciousness so we could share Creation, you were given the blessing of Free Will. Unfortunately, this blessing contained an opposing risk—that of your choosing not to recognize yourselves as Love. As you know, this is what happened. As it happened, you moved further from Me vibrationally. Your energy slowed. You chose to turn away from My reminder of who you are, and a part of your being was left empty.

Ah, you can feel My sadness and distress. My heart then began to contain anti-Love, the opposite; what you can call the enemy. Because all life is conscious, this anti-Love, being a part of Me, also has consciousness. Many call this Lucifer, and some of you believe that he himself made the choice to turn away from Me. But in truth, My beloved ones, it was you, in your Free Will, who abdicated your place as cells of only Love. You chose to look elsewhere other than to Me to understand who and what you were. Dichotomy, the two parts, good and evil, was thus born and moved forth into manifestation.

Ultimately, My heart is still Love. I know this, and when you are close to Me, so do you. But, as was our agreement, in service to your growth, I have allowed your choices to stand, and all of Creation has watched for the results.

This is very simplistic. As you expand in your awareness you will understand much more, but this will serve for Me to show you the things you need to know right now.

Each cell of My heart is huge, but however large, it is a definite size. Thus your being, though it can ultimately contain universes, is defined by the parameters of a cell of

My heart, so there is a finite opening through which energy comes. As you decide to re-embrace your truth as a being of Love, a portal for Love to flow through, you will refill the cell with light. Then, seeing your way, you will reclaim your essence of Love. The moment you do this—to the extent you do this—anti-Love ceases to exist in that cell. Please do your best to digest this. Thus, the opening used for the consciousness of anti-Love to pour energy through Creation is closed. It is not useable. It is returned to health. This is the healing of My heart—the return of My children.

Now remember I told you that the further away you are from Me, naturally, the more difficult it is for you to remember that you are Love. Since anti-Love is the complete opposite of Love (listen), its most powerful point, its strength, is the farthest away from Me. This can be explained vibrationally more accurately, but the idea of distance works very well and may be more accessible.

So the farther away from Me you are and the slower you vibrate, the more powerful is anti-Love. Love is the highest vibration. This is truth. The lowest vibration really is "the lie."

Now, because all Creation has consciousness, this anti-Love does also. There is a piece here that I can't fully explain to you yet, for your minds can't yet grasp it. But I'll mention this because it is important. *The energy of anti-Love really has no power at all. It is a lie. An illusion is what we call it. But more importantly (oh, please hear this!), the only real power it has is the power you give it.* For in truth, dear ones, it is a part of your being. (This is what I said would be difficult for you to grasp at this level, yet if you can, it is so important, even if you catch one tiny glimpse.)

So, of course, this anti-Love lie, this "black hole"

that exists where your Love is not present, wants you to keep giving it energy. Now this energy is a negative energy on the scale of life. The best way at present to describe it to you is as a "black hole." Since it only can come through into Creation because you have abdicated a certain portion of yourself as the cell in My heart, and because it lives solely on energy fed to it and has none of its own, it will do anything to keep you feeding it. To feed it you must believe in it, and therefore not fully remember that you are Love.

Because of your Free Will (humanity as a whole), you are here at a slow vibration living in a world that is essentially anti-Love. If it were not, darkness or anti-Love would not exist. It does exist because it is being fed by humanity and allowed to come into existence by humanity as well.

Now, many of you have asked Me how to deal with Evil—how to see it, how to relate to it and how to overcome it. These principles are of the utmost importance for you to understand. *The only way that darkness, evil, or anti-Love will cease is for you, each and every human being, to return your entire being to Love.* When you remember your truth, you will revitalize the dead area in your cell in My heart. Once revitalized, Love can again pour through you. And once the entirety of your SoulMate being is conscious Love, you have eliminated your share of darkness in the world.

Dear ones, all of you, if you can hear even a little of this, you can change the world. You can immediately do what you are meant to do. It is you who will light the world. It is you who will lift the world and humanity into the Golden Age.

Now as you are growing in your consciousness, you can start by recognizing that every time you focus on negativity in any form you are giving the anti-Christ energy. I have used the term anti-Love until now, but, of course, Christ is the name of My Love. ***Thus now you know what the anti-Christ is. It is the anti-Love. It is the negative energy that exists from the places where humanity has no Love. It is the parts of each human where they have forgotten their identity and left a hole where darkness can come through.***

So now I call you to come Home, back into your true relationship with Me, as the entry point in My heart through which My Love moves forth into manifestation. "Turn back to Love," I say to you, in all of your waking moments and in your dreams. As you recognize My call, ***you ask Me how to deal with the darkness you see around you.***

YOU MUST WITHDRAW YOUR ENERGY FROM IT. You must recognize your responsibility, and you must turn back to Me. From absolutely every perspective on every level of life, dear ones, do not engage it. ***Do not fight it, seek to destroy it or overcome it. If you do, the moment you put your attention on it, you are feeding it and giving it life.***

As you place your attention on darkness you are not seeing yourself. You can only remember who you are by looking at Me, for you are made in My image. You are cells in My heart and the closer we become, the closer you draw to Me, the easier and easier it is to remember who you are. ***ONLY IN THAT REMEMBRANCE WILL EVIL BE ERASED***, for in remembrance you will fill your being with My Love and you then become an opening for Love, and not for the anti-Christ.

I have often told you that where you put your attention is what you create. This is true on the deepest levels of All That Is. So the moment your attention is completely on Love, you have closed the hole in My heart created when your attention was withdrawn.

The SoulMate relationship is a critical piece of this re-awakening, for together you create your one cell of My heart, so you **both** must remember, and the fastest and most direct way to see who you think you are is to look at your relationship. Your SoulMate not only will reflect this to you, but you remind each other of your truth. As you awaken to the presence of your SoulMate, you are regaining your divine consciousness. Your SoulMate is your Love embodied before you, as I have repeatedly told you. Thus you can learn perfectly whether or not you are allowing My Love to flow through you. Without My Love flowing out from My heart, the system cannot be cleansed. It is Love flowing that brings the toxins up and out and revitalizes the lifeblood of Creation.

This is the answer to your question. *You can acknowledge that there is an anti-Christ, an energy and vibration that is the manifestation of anti-life (life without Love), but that is all!* Otherwise, keep your eyes, heart and mind focused upward on Me. Call continually for your Love to reclaim the all of your being, and accept your SoulMate. Manifest this outpicturing of your true reality and use this relationship. Use it to see every area where you are not choosing Love. Use it to consciously lift, lift, and lift the attention of humanity out of the illusion and into the truth. Please understand that you are a miniature heart, a portal, for pumping Love through Creation, and for delivering any contaminants picked up to the correct beings for cleansing.

It is true that the anti-Christ energy (and consciousness, for all things are embodied, even this) does want to do all it can to pull your attention to it. As you know, its single greatest tool is fear. However, it is not just active fear. It is lack of Love, for Love is a dynamic energy that fills up your being. You know your saying that nature abhors a vacuum? It is true. *Lack of Love is an opening for negativity, for darkness, as much as overt attention to the consciousness/manifestations of darkness. Please ponder this.* It is lack of Love that allowed evil to manifest. Lack of Love is anti-Love. The Bible expressed it as it not being acceptable to be lukewarm. *You must all be actively loving to be who you really are.* And, dear ones, as you come closer to Home you will learn that lack of Love becomes ever more subtle. Yet, as you come Home, you will be closer to Me, and I am always showing you who you are. All you have to do is look.

Thus I ask you to place before you every possible vision of Me. There is no neutral ground. Feed yourselves. Grow yourselves and seek every minute of every day to truly and fully grasp who you are as a being of Love. Do not deny the existence of darkness, for what you resist and especially what you fear, you are giving energy. You cannot resist darkness, dear ones, and your prayer every moment must be not to fear darkness either.

Now that you understand this, it is up to you to choose Love—to close the portal of your being to anti-Love by filling it completely with Love. *No, you cannot ever succumb to the battle of light and dark. Oh, that is where humanity is robbed of its identity! For in taking it on, you, the co-creators of the universe, say its name and feed it your power.* In other words, you create it. It is difficult for you to see from your level of current function-ing, but as I am, so are you too, the beginning and the end. Thus, at the same time that darkness is enticing you at your lowest level, dear ones, it flows into existence at your higher level, too. Not your highest level, for there you are united with Me. But at the level of our unified choice for your Free Will, you allow the anti-Christ into existence. Then at the level of illusion, or more accurately, hypnosis, you are tricked into fueling its existence by lending it your co-creative energy by fighting it!

Let this speak to your soul, for your mind may not comprehend. Yet your mind must be directed by you and by your Will to choose Love in absolutely everything. Only so are you turning your beautiful faces Homeward.

As you acknowledge the existence of the extremely large consciousness of darkness, or illusion, it will certainly seek to detain you, to draw you into the illusion. This is where you are tested. This, then, is your final stand—not in some far away place or time, but here in the little things of your daily life.

You must not let it in. Don't deny its existence but don't let it in. If it comes knocking, deny it entrance. Change the subject. Change the channel. *If you give it any attention, dear ones, you give it power and you absolutely give it entrance into your life.*

You must choose Love whenever and wherever "the lie" raises its head. You must raise yourselves above fear. When you do there will be no resonance for darkness within you. Then, my beloveds, nothing will ever again take your gaze off of Me.

Your success is assured, for Love is who you are. It is the remembering of this that is your path Home. Call for assistance, for you have so many who help you. Your ascension begins in earnest when you give your lives to Me, when Love becomes your highest priority. Let nothing change your mind.

It is the beginning.
It is now the
"walk to the New World"
for humanity.
Two thousand years ago,
it was one man.
His seed has taken root,
in ways you can't even imagine.
Thus, the Christ of God goes forth.
The seed now comes to harvest.
Dear ones,
only as you can be harvested
– uprooted, cut away from the old –
will you be ready for the new.

The Difference Between
Discernment and Judgment

*T*oday I speak to you about discernment vs.
judgment. When you can look at a given situation or a
being in question from the place of divine Love and purity,
dear ones, then you can assess what you are really seeing.
For lack of a better way to explain this, ***when you are filled
with the feeling you have when you see a wounded baby
animal, then you can move forward to help.***

My beloveds, I love you so much. I love you with a
Love that aches for you. I love you with a tenderness that
loves every eyelash and the way it curls upon your cheek. I
love you with a Love that cherishes every decision for Love
completely. I love you so totally that when you make a
decision for Love, it is no less celebrated than a world ruler
signing an accord for peace.

***Judgment is a process of the ego. Discernment is a
process of the heart.*** The heart always supports Love. The
heart always brings forth Love—in every move, every
thought and deed. Dear ones, the heart always seeks the
outcome of Love, of good, of grace, of service and especially
of the opening to the light, the opening to Love. Love is
patient and kind. Love will wait for "good to gather" to
support the outcome of Love.

***Discernment, dear ones, always sees a path to an
outcome of Love.*** Discernment is a heavenly view.
Discernment is lifted up. It is your "God Self" looking. It
is the awareness of your life within Me, and it looks forth

from that view. The discerning self is a self that is fulfilled, a self nourished in My Love so fully that all that you seek is to give forth Love. ***Discernment is your Love overflowing to another, asking, "how may I be of assistance here?"***

Judgment is your ego self and whether you like to see it or not, the ego loves self-righteousness. Thus, judgment, however well disguised, sees self as better than. Judgment has no goal other than the judgment itself. Just as in your choices for Love or ego, so it is with discernment and judgment. Judgment creates separation.

Now I must deliver a warning. Judgment lends itself readily to disguise.   It will take rigorous honesty to catch your ego at work in this arena, especially as you move deeper into this work. Why? If you are in a situation to choose Love over ego, you can simply refuse your ego. You are protected from many possibilities for mistakes because it is either ego or not ego. But discernment can be more subtle and is absolutely critical to your success. It must be exercised all the days of your existence until you are fully re-united with Me. So there is no "cut and dried" picture. There is only discernment about discernment! (A sense of loving humor...)

I draw all of you close to Me. Very close. I show you My Love, right here, directly. I show you also My Love for you as it manifests in the form of your beautiful SoulMate, and I tell you that every moment of "practice" together is the most valuable thing you can ever do. Every moment of clearing yourself, of opening your heart and of sharing together the experience of true Love, of purity of Love and purpose. Oh, My beloved ones, please look into the mirror, the mirror of your SoulMate. For those whose Soul Mate has not manifested, I ask that you open to them on the inner level, and that you look then at the mirror of your life.

Look to Me to teach you discernment. This is very important. Only I can show you what is true about any human being. Dear ones, you do not know what they have been through! You do not know what their work has been on the inner planes. The person you are looking at could be ready to "blast off" tomorrow. How, then, could you judge them today? Yet you can and you must discern where service will assist them. Discern where they need your prayer energy, then PRAY. Right then! I say this adamantly because *discernment is not complete without a loving outcome, an action that leads to Love.* Please absorb this, because this is the key, the key to the world's awakening as humanity understands this, and the key to completion of the circuit in which you are a part.

Beloved ones, if you discern and do not act to create movement toward an outcome of Love, it is like standing in the dark with your hand on the light switch but never turning it on! The circuit is not complete. Because it is more blessed to give rather than to receive, the blessing that is meant for you there will not be yours. And there's even more. When you complete this circuit of discernment and then the giving of energy toward an outcome of Love, your energy is woven into (or flows into) the other person or people's energy, thus elevating the vibration and connecting them to me.

Can you see how amazing this is? Can you see, for those of you who are dedicated to the transformation, dedicated to the manifestation of Love into the world, that this process is the way to accomplish your goals, to manifest your dreams? This is the way to bless all of those who are in need even as you live your days.

These things must become the way you think, the way you live, the way you feel, yourself. I tell you that this energy exchange is spiritual food in a form that will nourish you far more than anything you could draw to yourself or charge your food with. Why? Because it includes the blessed energy of giving. (May I say these words again? The blessed energy of giving.) This energy is the highest food available on Earth.

Dear ones, the fact that some of you are asking is a great and powerful thing. The fact that you are honing your actions, that you desire to have the greatest purity of thought as well as deed. This will continue to bring blessings to you. It will reveal to you on ever-deeper levels the steps toward greater and greater understanding.

The other part of this is about light, about vibration, about recognizing the energy at which something is operating. This will become a language in itself. At first, it will take a high level of effort to maintain your lives at a higher vibratory level. This is absolutely worth every effort. Oh, dear ones, this is the missing key that you are now turning in the lock. This is something that surpasses the ego (if you use it honestly, of course). Once you learn to truly assess vibrational energy, you will be speaking the heart's language. Love has a clear signature in all Creation. It is known by all beings. It is honored by every heart. This is true. Some hearts may be blocked off by ego, but the moment the heart is free, the energy, the vibration of Love is not only recognized but responded to instantly.

I ask all of you now to begin a dedication to the awareness of vibrational energy that is to guide you through all the rest of your life. Life should be written there with a capital "L" because I'm speaking of your REAL LIFE, your eternal life.

I will send each of you examples of energy shifts, vibrational levels – and the thoughts that precipitated them. It now becomes imperative that you recognize that every thought totally affects your energy, especially as you become more attuned to the light.

I begin to offer forth
the vision of your future,
for I have confidence.
And well I should!
Dear ones,
I have confidence in My own heart!
That heart is you.
So of course I know that Love
will now arrive in full measure.
Love will now become your truth.
Oh, not only your truth
in these limited areas of your consciousness
you now see as yourselves
— oh, no.
Your truth as you step forth to claim
your heritage that Jesus held forth to you.
With this age it now becomes your truth,
not only his.

Mastery

*T*he topic now is Mastery—Mastery of your Will, Mastery of your ego and the Mastery of your service. You have heard this term most of your life, and you have a vague awareness of its higher significance. I want to show you how, by your Love and your intention, you become the blood vessels and the nerves of My Love's embodiment. As you open to your Mastery of the lower worlds, the vibration of illusion, the density, then you do truly become a channel for Love and a channel for light in a way that creates in the most real way the body of Christ, of which you are a living part.

It is really only in your acceptance of your role as a part of this body that you will finally be in alignment with your destiny. Alignment with your destiny only comes by giving. The practice of giving forth creates new vessels in the body of Christ—just as exercise creates new blood vessels in a physical body. Just as a physical body will create additional vessels to circumvent any blocked blood vessels, so too does this work spiritually. As you raise yourselves up to the level of connectedness, then you will be able to join with others to create a flow of new life energy for the whole being that is humanity, the being that is My heart.

How you come to be a part of this new life, a vessel for this new energy is to go beyond the smaller self in service. "Of course!" you say. "I know this." But do you live this? That is the question. Even many who are very filled with light still have the main part of their daily focus on themselves. If not on themselves, the focus is on the physical world and its emotional and mental counterparts.

Many of you have said to Me many times, with deepest devotion, that you serve the awakening of humanity. Yet your attention is drawn in to the "daily work" consistently, dear ones. Yes, the daily work at this time must be done, but Mastery is the ability to see the result, the spiritual truth before you always. *You must know Love's great truth as you answer the phone. You must love with your consciousness fully engaged while you do all that your daily life places before you.*

Dear ones, here is what you should know. Mastery is taking everything in your life to its highest spiritual level and living with it there—living with it there until nothing else is your reality at all. You will still be able to function in your daily life, but as you do, you will become more and more aware of all that is occurring.

Mastery is about claiming your power, yes. But it is even more than this. Mastery is taking the suffering you experience and living it in Christ. It is taking the interactions with others and doing the same. *It is taking the smaller self out of the equation.* Mastery, dear ones, is bringing all things into obedience to your higher Will. Not your day-to-day mind, but, as the Bible says, "The mind that was in Christ Jesus." May this be your current prayer, your mantra for this time in your life.

Many of you are ready to take your positions as a Master. And what does this mean but becoming the Master of your life. When you speak of Ascended Masters, you acknowledge that it includes some form of Mastery to attain such a title. But you have not put much thought into it. Now, standing on the threshold of your own Mastery, this turning point of your spiritual growth, Mastery of your life is the key to this door.

Now, let Me tell all of you this. It is not that you do

not own this level of Mastery in your beings, acquired together in your eons of dedicated service. *It is that you must now bring this level of Mastery quickly into full expression in your current lives in order to allow My Love to flow through you.*

You cannot be the blood vessels of the body of Christ rushing Love to every part of the body that needs it, unless you are fully aware of that body at every moment. You cannot be the nerve cells, firing off the electricity of light, the sparks of energy that will ignite the wholeness of humanity, unless you are aware of your position in the larger body.

You are ready to make every breath a breath of service —every thought a thought of the action on humanity of Love and light. I want your vision to be so high, so clear, that you will be able to know how much Love you were able to deliver to each and every person with whom you have any contact at all. Not only this, but how many other people were impacted by your delivery of Love. How many family members of that person you spoke with? How many co-workers in the office from which they called?

As you begin to interact in an openly spiritual manner with more and more people, you will be able to touch, to deliver Love to a phenomenal number of people. This is training for you. I want you to be so aware of My Love flowing through you that you will build an entire "language" to describe these energy experiences—whether the Love was received when working with everyone and whether the light is received when working with those who are aware.

In order to function like this, *you must master all lower vibration energies in you and in your life.* You must be a "transformation center" and be fully functional. You must be living ever more consciously in the Christ light and seeing yourself as a true part of "the mind that was in Christ Jesus"—without a trace of ego.

As you become the Master of all the energies within you, everything is lifted to the Christ Mind. In doing so, you then transform everything you came forward to transform and use it in service to humanity every moment.

Let me give you an example. Recall a particularly painful experience from your life. Before you are two choices. You can open the memories and allow them to flood back over you and you can "hope for the healing that you need." Or you can choose to see with "the mind that was in Christ Jesus." You can choose Mastery and in so doing transform your sorrows into the Love of Christ for the world.

There is more energy released by a turn when someone shifts direction, from say, darkness to light, from selfishness to giving, from fear to trust and Love. The energy released as a consciousness turns back to Me (in whatever area is represented in their life, whatever area needs Mastery). This is the gift of the shift to Christ Mind! So every single area where you have held negativity or limitation, when released and transformed through your change in awareness, gives off a "push of energy" that launches both personal and planetary transformation.

As you stand here on this point on your path, you can see how much is to be gained by your Mastery—the Mastery of every limitation in every possible form. You can see that there is a bonus given if you can turn around. Thus every suffering becomes a gift. Every doubt becomes a blessing. Every sacrifice becomes a glory. A glory of Love. Please seek to deeply understand this. In this, dear ones, you become a disciple of Christ yourself, for this Mastery was the heart of what Jesus taught as he became the embodiment.

This Mastery is the hallmark of every true Christed being.

So, yes, a Christ does, very often, take on humanity's suffering in order to raise it up by "seeing it" through the Christ mind, thus delivering its gift of energy for the upliftment/transformation of humanity.

The suffering of Jesus was brought into service of Christ. The suffering of Mary was brought into service of Christ by the awareness of the truth, by holding that vision of truth or perfection while experiencing the suffering. *It is true that Mary's ability to hold the truth perfectly in her mind, regardless of the suffering, made the Resurrection successful.*

There is no longer need (or time!) for counseling in the traditional sense. People must now come to Me. This awakening, this transformation, is the only thing that works now, as we move into humanity's awakening. Do you realize what important information this is? It is based on the truth —*where your attention is, is what you create.* So those counseling on difficulties are actually creating more difficulties. But those looking to the spiritual solution will be creating their only real healing, their only possibility for awakening.

It is that which is subjugated to the highest vision that becomes a part of who you are. Your truth is that you are part of My heart. So as you recognize this, you will then be able to keep with you the transformed connections that are the bridge, as you become the vessels for feeding the body of Christ.

I will teach you more—how to open into this awareness of Mastery, how to bring your experiences of this life into residence in your true being, so that what you have learned and what you have remembered work together to expand your vision, and to create your experiences as part of the One.

Choose Love, dear ones.
Choose Love.
In every moment.
As the heart becomes the instrument
through which you live your life,
I promise you will be immersed in joy,
regardless of what is happening in the world.
And as you choose to see Love,
so do you also create Love
and thus, in every moment
you also free the world.

The Light Illuminates the Darkness. Expanding Consciousness

Oh, I am here, and I joyously await the day when you are here with Me as much as I am here with you! Please hurry. Hurry and turn your beautiful eyes and your loving hearts around to face Me. Open to the glorious presence of Love in the world and make this your reality. ***It is true that what you place before your holy power of attention is what will manifest.*** It is true that what you accept in your heart as your possibility is what you become. Thus I await with joyous anticipation the time when you realize that it is just as easy to live in the light. It is easy to live in fog, and it is even easier to experience the bliss of Love as your day-to-day reality.

At present you still believe that there is somewhere you must go, something different that you must be in order to live in My presence, to blossom in these arms of Love. All the while I am whispering to you, "but this is what you are—this Love, this beauty!"

Right now you believe you must lift your vibration in order to truly hear Me, and it certainly does seem this way. But soon, dear ones, soon you will realize that you expend far more energy to keep yourselves from flying to Me. You will come to see that everything here in this current human reality is designed to use your own energy to keep you away from Me. Then ***you will see that all you have to do is remember who you are and all the rest will fall away.*** When it does, you will have all the energy you need to completely re-make the world. You have that energy, that light, that Love and that power already in you, awaiting freedom from the cage of false beliefs.

You do not need to teach others to focus on what is wrong, what needs to be healed. However, (listen, because this is very important) when the light is turned on, it will, absolutely and without fail, reveal all that has been held in darkness. Thus, all those whom you teach, you must also teach to have the strength of personal honesty, for when someone chooses the light they will be given their freedom. They will gain their spiritual wings. But they will also be left facing all that the light will reveal, and it may not be pretty. Yet with the light, with My transforming Love, it can easily be uplifted. The learning can be accomplished and it can become the strength in your wings.

This is why we have been speaking of spiritual Mastery. Do you see how perfectly everything fits together? Not only what you are learning but what others around you need to learn also. *Spiritual Mastery is the ability to look at everything and to bring it into the light with you.* Please remember this statement, dear ones. It is what is now waiting in front of this nation as well as in front of individuals. It is the strength to acknowledge everything that the light reveals and then courage to take it to the light. It is the courage to come to Me with any weakness and any strife, anything within you that is not perfect light, and to ask Me to help you transform it. This is the healing. Because seeing something without the light to illuminate and transform it is creating more of the same. It is using the power of your attention, even if unconsciously, thus giving it life. Giving it your life, for as your attention is, so is your energy.

Mastery means the strength of spirit that it takes to acknowledge and then transform all within you that is not perfect harmony. So when you give these gifts of illumination forth to others, and as you learn and grow yourself, you must be aware that light must be given to everything and the darkness then revealed must be transformed.

Every lesson in the world now is spiritual. Everything must be approached this way. This does not mean there is no place for counselors. It means that they must only serve as midwives at the birth of spiritual Mastery over all that is revealed in the light.

As you begin to see what is in your subconscious mind, you are brought face-to-face with the dark forces that have plagued you. Now you must continually hold your goal of transformation into your spiritual fullness, and everything brought before you will ultimately release its energy back into your consciousness for you to use with awareness—awareness of what brought you to this point. It will be awareness of the gift of your challenge and most importantly, awareness of the gift of service that will come from your Mastery in this area.

So it is not that there is no "work on yourself," especially since growth is the hallmark of My presence in your life. *It is that everything is subject to the spirit. Everything. Thus (pay attention!) the only place that has your attention is the light. Your illumination. The truth. Spiritual awakening.* As you place Me at the pinnacle of your life you will see that everything you look upon, you will always see for its spiritual side, its message, the way it will grow you, how your light can shine when it is removed, released, transformed.

In traditional therapy, the focus is on "what is wrong with you." Yet these same things, when revealed as part of your spiritual journey, are understandings of how to lead others Home—energy released to assist you to serve, awareness of areas in which the light must be fully introduced. So the learning will continue. It must. If it does not, then you are not alive spiritually. But the learning is always in the context of the expansion of your light and your opportunity to serve.

The light is increasing. This, of course, you know. Dear ones, as it does, it will reveal what has been hidden. Truly this is what was happening on September 11, 2001 in New York City with the World Trade Center. The consciousness of the United States has refused to acknowledge many things on both sides of the "terrorist equation" — things about money, and the practices, internationally, of manipulation of money by the few. On the other side, of course, the United States has completely failed to acknowledge the killing that has gone on in the name of both "democracy" and money (including that international manipulation).

Thus what happened truly was the result of the light that is pouring into the Earth and into the mass consciousness of humanity. At this moment, obviously, that consciousness and the governments of the countries involved, have not chosen honesty. Thus, the light will continue to bring forth the results of this now rejected awareness. Now the rejection itself will also need transforming.

So in your personal lives, as you open more and more fully to Me, dear ones, you must be willing to see all that the light reveals. You must be willing to do this all the way up the vibrational scale. This means that as you become more and more clear, the revelations of the light will get more and more precise. As your vibrational reality rises, as you become clearer light, more light, a speck of darkness will cause as much of a problem as a huge infringement did in the past. This is because you are now working in such refined energy that your attention has far more power to manifest things. So that little "speck" will come forth as a boulder on your path more readily than a boulder-size blockage used to do. Thus I call for total dedication and total Mastery.

It is also true that *you are the "way showers," the path finders, creating the new nerve connections in the brain of the wholeness of humanity and the Earth.* Thus you are laying down completely new pathways, and your personal journeys do need to leave traceable steps for others behind you to follow.

See everyone who comes to you needing assistance as a chance to implement the sharing that is the purpose of your lives. I want you to ask to be guided to serve those who need the information, by giving it to them freely. Nothing is more important than a person's spiritual life. *Anything we can give forth together to attune any heart more finely to My Love is worth every effort.*

You can, and must, order your world according to your Will. This is a step in your Mastery program, which, of course, includes manifesting what you need. However, remember, you are taking the Christ pattern up to the level appropriate for entrance by humanity into the New World. What this means is that your lives will tell the story of how to get there. This means that you will be going a "longer way" than you might personally need to, because you will be teaching others and the others must understand how you got there.

I ask each of you to S-T-R-E-T-C-H even more than you already are. Be sure to avoid looking at your lives as "how much I'm expected to manage" and rather always see it as an opportunity to shift your consciousness—to see how much more you are than you ever thought you could be. Place your attention on the blessing of great service, the opportunity to remember your Mastery (for truly you are Masters. Certainly you all must suspect this of yourselves by now.) And I ask you to flip the context in which you see everything into the view from the spirit, rather than the view from the personality

Choose carefully what you watch on television, for, dear ones, as you keep growing you must realize, truly realize the power of your attention every moment and the value of cleanliness of mind and emotion. Every time you watch killing or other negativity, it is like a bruise on your consciousness of light, and of course your attention reinforces anything. So at least I ask you to affirm your reality and use the power of the light to transform negativity if you find yourselves watching these things. Please see that they are an expression of the mass consciousness, and as such they can serve you as entry points where you can inject positive energy into the mass mind.

Remember that you are always looking for a crack through which to pour Love. Movies and television offer that opening into the current mass consciousness of humanity. So whatever you are witness to, real events or fiction, be sure to use it.

I am always lifting and illuminating you. Let this light then shine forth to illuminate the world.

Dear ones,
claim the Christ that is in you.
As you do, this will call forth
that very light in all you see —
for your recognition is everything.
You are the co-creators of Love.
Blessed ones,
what you name in your thoughts
and fuel in your feelings
becomes so.

To Be Christed is to Know Only Love

When I come to you, you will always know because you will feel your heart expand. You will feel the Love that is within you reach forth to become the Love that is without. You will know then that we are in true communion. This experience of Love is all I want to give you. Why? Because once you know this Love you understand that this is all there is.

When you are here, lifted into joy in My presence, when your heart becomes everything, when the kiss of the breeze is the signature of My holy breath, you will know that I speak to you as Love in all things.

There is only Love within you. There is only Love without. But this is not some abstract form of thought. It is as real an experience as the physical touch of your hand upon the pen, or your breath within your throat. As you grasp this truth of Love you will understand the path to your full awakening.

You must expand the Love within you until it manifests the Love without so clearly that you live every moment in absolute surety of this reality of Love. Not a doubt, not an experience of anything else.

When you become this filled with Love, dear ones, then for you, Love truly becomes all there is. At that point you have become Me. You have experienced the total truth of Love, for if Love is All That Is, and I am All That Is, then you and I are One. This then is when you are a Christed being.

This is when the illusion disappears and you know yourself as My heart. From this point, when you look at any other being, all you see is Love. Whether you are walking through what you would now deem "the pits of Hell" or you are residing with the "choirs of heaven," wherever you look, Love is what you see.

To be a Christ is to be fully alive to the truth of your existence as Love in Me. It is not that you give up your discernment, for even I can see when a being is not in alignment with Love. But dear ones, *when you become Christed beings, all you will see is the most tender Love. All you will feel is the joyous privilege of being able to touch one more piece of our great being.* Everything within you will reach forth in joy at the opportunity to reflect that Love back to the being who embodies it.

Thus if you are standing in that pit of hell and a tortured soul looks up at you, the Christed being, they will be wrapped in the warmth of your Love. They will be upheld in your vision of their truth rather than the illusion they are pretending to be. Such Love will pour from you, heart, soul, mind, body, so that if there is a crack in their armor, your Love will be through it instantly, winging its way to their heart, bringing light to the darkness of the hell they have lived in.

How can I tell you what it is like to love so completely that this Love is absolutely all you see? Are you getting glimpses of this? The greatest path to understanding Christ is the Love of your SoulMate. The SoulMate is the gift I have given you so you will always have My Love with you, so you will have proof of who you are, standing right before you. So you will have the perfect place to grow into the Christ that you are.

Becoming Christ is a relationship with Me. It is the

recognition by you of your divinity until all that you see is the truth of Love. It is written by My Will that this is what is next for you, My humanity, My beloved children, My very own heart coming alive within Me.

You know that what is called the "Second Coming of Christ" is the resurrection of humanity—from the mud into the Lotus, from the illusion into the truth. Once again you must recognize the gift, your heritage, and the fact that I have given you the mirror of your SoulMate that you could never forget the truth of my Love for you, because I have built the proof right into your being.

Beloved ones, when you find your SoulMate, when you let go of the illusion and see them standing before you, I want you to know that in them I am standing before you. In them you get to relate to a living, breathing manifestation of My Love—of who you are. It is truly as if you can look at them with this open heart and even the illusion that they are separate from you will fall away—the illusion that they can possibly want anything else but Love. Please. Rise above the words here. Please feel the joy of the open heart embracing your beloved only to find that it is Me who is there, loving you perfectly as you become ever more able to accept My Love. It is only you who is there accepting the truth of your being.

True Love is the Holy Trinity of this New Age. It is no different. Father, Son and Holy Spirit is exactly the same as God, man, and woman, for what is the Holy Spirit but the intuition, the breath of wisdom and inspiration that is the feminine?

Beloved ones, please take these gifts I have for you. Become the candles of the lighted SoulMates that will illuminate the world. It is the joyful experience of Love manifesting that will lift all of you beyond illusion.

Now I will tell you this (again). **Love is the only answer.** The only healing is the upliftment of hearts into their truth of Love. As I will your awakening, it becomes imperative (as you know) that you do understand consciousness. You must honor every person's truth so much that you offer no other proof of anything other than the fact that they are Love. I ask you to trust their recognition of this to bring them into harmony with truth — their truth and Mine, which is the same.

As you learn to open your hearts so completely that the illusion disappears, you will recognize ever more easily that such recognition is the only answer. And if you explain to others that the spiritual path will bring the SoulMate, without fail, I have another promise to give to you. There may be an ego that will try to block the way to this truth, but that person's heart will never forget your words. Their heart, every heart, knows this truth, and now added to this, I am calling, calling for the awakening of every heart.

There are many exciting things to learn. And there is turmoil in the outer world as the light stirs up that which is anti-light and reveals its presence. You have understood that you must hold the highest vision, the highest good. *I affirm for you again that for human beings that highest truth, that greatest good is the presence of the SoulMate. As you each come to accept yourselves as Love, so that Love will become embodied.*

Your SoulMate is My Love in the form that you can feel and touch. It is the form that will always be the proof of My Love, the proof of My consciousness in every part of you. My first recognition as I willed Creation was My need for a reflecting consciousness—a way to see who I am. Dear ones, that is the reason for Creation. Thus, recognizing this truth, the very first thing that I willed was that I might know My own heart, that My heart know itself — self awareness of My nature, My Love. Thus, every cell in My heart became self aware, able to reflect its truth to itself, within itself—SoulMates.

Of course, My dearest ones, there is no end to My Love or the possibility of understanding it. This I want you to say forth in joy—there is no end to the growth of awareness of SoulMates. No end to the ever-deepening experience of Love. Do you see how the ego has corrupted this truth? It has stolen from humanity the commitment needed to stay in holy marriage, holy relationship in order to focus enough attention on Love to reveal the SoulMate.

We must find every way to unite hearts in dedication to Love, to real Love, because Love will take people through all the rest easily. It will transform, in its beautiful flames, all that is not Love. For anyone you long to bless, anyone you long to heal, I promise that true Love will heal everything. All "affliction" and all negativity is the illusion. Love, as you know, brings clarity. Even those who are living transformers as are many of you—it is Love that will do the transforming. So everything that comes to your awareness can be gently placed in your shared SoulMate heart to lift it to its highest.

As this experience of Love within you and without becomes stronger and clearer, the illusion gets "sandwiched" between until it really will fade from your view. This is how I want it to be. As you learn more about the movement or the forces or process of co-creation, dear ones, there cannot be anything else in your consciousness. You are becoming vortexes of creative power.

For this last part, I want to lift you higher and higher to speak with you each now individually. In speaking of Mastery and now speaking of what it means to be Christed beings, I remind you. When you are seeing truth as the foreground, you will not even have need of discernment.

Why? Because there will be nothing in you that is not Love. Oh, My beloved ones, allow Me to show you how it feels to love My children SO much that everything they do is fine because you know who they are. You know that they are in eternity, right here in My heart.

You know that this time of exploration really is as if you sent your own children to a movie. That's it. One piece of one evening. Do you worry overly even if your children see a horror movie? You do not because you have the perspective of the percentage of their lives that movie amounts to. And so do they. So even if they are so scared they have to rush to the bathroom and be sick, later they will be laughing about it with their friends.

This is the foreground/background picture. The foreground is eternity. It is the absolute assurance of success. Your children and Mine (all of you) are Love finding itself. You are Love discovering what it is NOT, learning what it is. Now, in this time of awakening, people are going to begin to compare notes about the movies. "Oh, don't see the one about low self-esteem. It's awful!" "Be very careful if you go into the theater of self-deception. It seems to go on forever!" So very quickly people will realize that they can choose what "movie of life" they want to see. Some of you will go into the theater with them and gently turn on the lights. Thus people won't have to wait until they've gone through the whole movie before they can choose to upgrade.

You who engage in this work, which certainly could be viewed as negative or difficult, will be given the great blessing of understanding what it means to be Christed. Before you will be held up a vision of pure Love that will lift you easily so all of your work will be done from the level of the greatest good, the highest light, the most pure Love. Please take in what this means. It means that you are drawing this into your lives. You will be coming together in

48

the highest energy available here on Earth. I do not need to tell you there is no place for ego here.

Dear ones, you have a much bigger picture—not only to see but to paint for humanity. Every time someone reads one of these Messages, the energy of this vision is planted in them. If it is nourished at all, it will grow and they will be back for more. The "code" for the new human DNA is the joined double helix of the SoulMate. But every understanding, even unconscious, is of great importance.

Remember I have told you that you must be ever vigilant for every tiny crack, every opening in every person? Now you can see how you can "feed the Love" into those cracks through the Love that I am placing in every word upon these pages, amplified by the open hearts of all of you.

I place into your hands and hearts the gift of My Love. It is beyond your minds to analyze but your hearts have no problem.

Whenever you are exposed to the illusion, to rifts of ego, to stories of war—the entire garment of separation, turn to your SoulMate and use your Love to lift it to the true reality. You will begin to experience that reality more and more, thus being ever more able to deliver the blueprint to everyone easily.

I will bring you more light and more Love as I bless My beloved children through you who have offered yourselves.

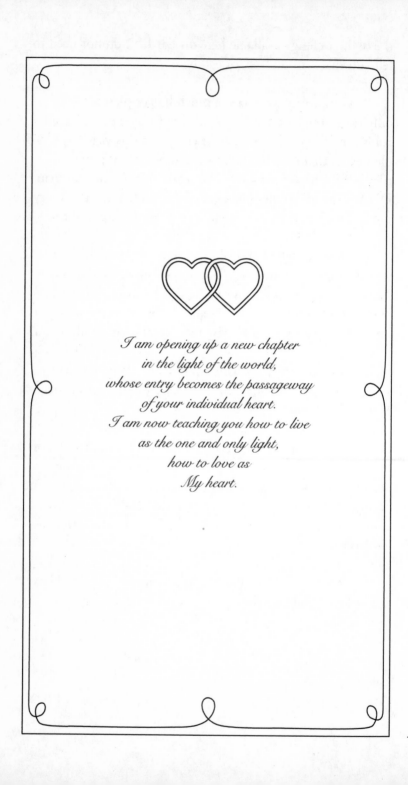

I am opening up a new chapter
in the light of the world,
whose entry becomes the passageway
of your individual heart.
I am now teaching you how to live
as the one and only light,
how to love as
My heart.

Shifting from the Ego to the Heart

I am here, lifting you in the joy of Love. I show you again that the only truth is that which you can perceive with the heart. Truly, the heart is the single eye by which the truth of Love is forever revealed. *Until you see only with the heart as your instrument of sight, you will experience the shadows as well as the light.* It is a misperception. It is searching for truth with double vision as if you were walking through life with your eyes crossed.

As long as you see with the eyes of duality, you will be subject to the results of that seeing. If you are seeing with the eyes of duality, looking at life through both the heart *and* the ego, then as you rise in a column of light, so, too, is there ever and always a corresponding and equal column of shadow. And if your vibration takes a "dip," if something sneaks through the cracks of your armor of Love, then you will be subject to this darkness, simply because you believe it.

Beloved ones, no matter what you do, no matter how much time you spend lifting in Me in Love, if you are in duality it will never be permanent. It will never be all you see, your only experience. The Garden of Eden is happening this moment—this Now and this Now and this. As long as you are standing under the tree of good *and* evil, you will always experience the darkness again.

Yes, you know all of this—but do you know it with such conviction that nothing can change your mind? No, not yet but you will. There will come a time soon when your heart becomes your only truth. What this means, beloved ones, is that you will go to stand beneath the Tree of Life, returning at last to the point where "we left off." You will return to the point where I held you in My Love and you were strong in your glory, your precious individuality. It is the point where you knew that you were unique in all Creation, and yet you also knew that you are only Love.

Oh, beloved ones, all of you whose hearts recognize My call, you can, and must, remember that the only way that you can know yourself is through your heart. Can you see this? If you look at yourself through the eyes of duality, even from the aspect of "good," you will always see the shadow there as well. It will be the shadow of a false perception, the shadow of the belief that there are two powers in this world. *That is the illusion, truly, in a nutshell.* A shadow has no substance. Surely you can recognize this, even by looking at the physical world. Dear ones, this is the truth of darkness, of evil, of all the shadow substance that has come from only one thing—the blockage of the light that is your own belief in the power of a shadow.

Dear ones – every one of you – the Tree of Life is made of light. It casts no shadow. Beneath it there is no darkness. Rather, as you look upon it, you will see the miracle that the Tree of Life is you. Single of purpose, born of only light, the "sap" of the Tree is the living substance of Love. As you understand this, you will know there is only one truth and only one power—that of Love.

You must now make it your mission to "uncross your eyes," to become able to see in, with, and through your heart. You must bring to you these experiences of the Tree of Life, the truth of the real world, which is heaven on Earth. To this end you must practice diligently. You must learn not to attempt to rise above when you are warring with the shadow but rather, learn how it will dissolve in the unity of heart. Learn to make your heart your only instrument now.

How will you do this? *By lifting daily to heart consciousness and view life from there.* Record for yourself the truth of what you see. Record in your consciousness who you really are—not seen from the level of duality but seen from the level of the truth. If at first this seems like imagination, do not worry. The heart doesn't lie. So you can trust that there is at least an element of truth in what your heart is sweetly dropping into your consciousness. For where did those imaginary tales come from that are the legends of the world? Unicorns and fairies and a glorious world of color, light, and beauty where Love always wins the day, where SoulMates are united and the prince will always find his bride? They came from your collective memory of the truth of the One Reality. There is beauty beyond current imagining, and every being who shares this world is alive in truth with you. All the inklings of change in the world, communication with animals and nature spirits— these are the glimpses from the heart as it now begins to stir within each human being.

So experiment every day. Ask your heart for the truth of the world. This includes the truth of you, of who you really are when the sunlight of Love is upon you and all shadows disappear. This, dear ones, is the new "therapy" — discovering the truth of the spirit, unearthing the glorious patterns of Love that you are, and taking that journey of Love with all your beautiful allies - the butterflies that lead the way, the birds that whisper your true Love's holy name, the vehicle of light that is your body, and the truth of Love that is your spirit.

This, dear ones, is using your Will to assist in the shift—to switch to the heart, not only when I lift you, but consciously choosing of your own volition the unity consciousness of Love.

Think how long you have been in training to believe in darkness. This should give you pause! So certainly it will make sense to train yourselves to see the truth from the perspective of your heart, which is the only way you can ever find it. Yes, your heart can then "rain into your mind" the light-filled images, the golden glow, the lift of spirit, the arrival of joy so great, so powerful that you can barely contain it.

You can do much to regain this consciousness of the unity of Love. You can also realize that looking at Love from the realm of duality is looking through the glass darkly, for duality is exactly thus. It is the "once-removed" perception —the very false belief that is the veil that separates you from all that is beyond this little pocket of Time and Space.

It does take focus. It does take energy expended on My behalf (and yours). It takes attention. It's exactly as if your eyes are crossed and you are seeing double (the world of good and evil). You must exert the effort and use the attention necessary to make your eyes uncross. I know you know the feeling of just letting your eyesight drift out of focus, becoming blurred or double. You have to decide to focus and your muscles then have to take the order from your Will. You can feel your muscles respond and your eyes shift position. Your vision comes back in focus. It is the same with switching to the heart. It is easier to be lazy, to allow your focus to drift, to see the blurry lines, and to see the shadow along with the light.

So, in truth, there is not an "equal and opposing force" of dark for the light you carry. It appears that way as long as you are looking at it through the eyes of dual consciousness, good and evil, light and dark. But when you exert the effort to focus the attention in the heart, there is only one force and that is Love. These things will begin to take hold in the consciousness of humanity.

So if you see and feel and experience those shadows, you must know that you have to switch to your heart. And through your loving Will, dear ones, you can wrap them in the one light and they will disappear, the shadows now transformed in the noon sun of your being.

Watch. You will begin to see, beloved ones. When you come into the consciousness of the heart, you will feel My presence, and there will be only Now, only Here, alive in the glorious expression of Love that we are. It will be tender, exalting, filled with deep knowledge of the "mansions of the Father," the truth of all the worlds and stars and lives, all the oceans of Love and all the rivers of being that are fed into it. Then out of this beautiful expansiveness will come our communion. Right here in the Now you will know yourself as My heart made manifest. You will know that right here within the vastness of your being is where I become visible as you, in you, a glorious expression so unique that you will know yourself.

Become only Love.
Share only Love together.
Then Love will be your reality.
Love will be completely who you are.
What you are.
Where you are.
Then you just experience
every perfect moment.

If Thine Eye Be Single.
Looking at the World Through
God's One Light

I am here with you. I surround you with beauty and with the voices of Nature. They are to tell you, continually, of My Love and of the great tenderness with which I made you and have always cared for you. They are to tell you of the lovely beauty of the Earth, your home here in this dimension, as she holds you in safety and nourishment.

Now I want to record a question that has come to Me and to talk of what you are learning. Why? Because this is THE most important area in all the areas of growth and study.

The question to Me is how you can live in this world as it is now being manifested and be present enough to truly hear and help others, without falling into a "dip" away from Me. The reason I have been asked this is that all of you have had the experience of being lifted to Me. In that reality there is only light. With Me you are like a star, pulsing out only light, rejoicing in great jubilation that you were understanding this law. *If thine eye be single, thy whole body will be filled with light.*

Yet all of you experience people coming to you, asking for help with heartbreak, with a view of the world far removed from this true reality. You are touching the reality of war in the world. The question then is how do you hold to that "single eye" in which you are living in the one true light, and at the same time be available to those you can assist?

My answer is this. When you know this great and shining Love as yours, once you know that this is all you want, once you have been here, in My arms in highest communion, I will assist you to turn back to the world. I will assist you to look upon what is happening from the one true light. As together we look through that light, you will be able to see how you can assist, how to see what is happening.

From this truth, dear ones, there is no fear. Thus (pay attention!) you have NO link to the pseudo reality at all. Your heart, your mind, your soul, the fullness of your being, all reside in the one light. Your eye is single. But just because your eye is single does not mean it doesn't see. It does see. But it sees the truth. It sees people struggling with the dark hand of fear. It sees the deceptions of those who have chosen to be anti-light. It sees manipulation, corruption and greed. *But even as it sees, it knows only Love.* And this, My beautiful ones, is how you can and must turn back to assist the world.

You know that fear is the greatest danger, and the greatest tool of those whose agenda is to destroy rather than create. You will love them. You will love those who are struggling in fear and you will love those who manipulate them. You will see those who are oppressed and those who oppress—and you will love the oppressors and the victims. You will know that neither one is truth. Your Love will pour upon them as everything you see reveals its truth to you.

As you come to see in Me, in the single eye of truth, your vision will be a beam of light that will penetrate the darkness and reveal to you what is held within. *No matter what you see, your response is only Love, for you will see duality from the light of oneness.* The darkness cannot hold sway. Rather, darkness must always give way to light. *Thus if you have no resonance to darkness within—*

darkness will reveal its truth.

Suddenly you will know who can be touched by our Love, Mine moving through you, and you will reach forth your hand. Soon you will see how to find the tiniest of cracks through which light can make its way in.

This is not rhetoric. This is spiritual principle. This is that to which I ask you to rise, to ascend. To claim your own light inside the beam of Mine because *I must be able to work through your hands, your hearts, minds and bodies. This is the only way that the strength of this light can be brought into the experience of this world.*

I do not ask you to turn away. Rather, I ask you to please be right there, in the thick of it—yet centered completely in the light of truth. If you can do this, I promise that your light will be like a laser, cutting through the thick fog of illusion, searching for the souls who are lost in the night.

You must have no fear. I need you. I need you to be able to walk through hell and see only Love. But this does not mean you can't see what hell is to those who are in it. Do you see the difference?

The success of the light is assured. I ask you to remember this. Here in your individual lives, and there, in every layer of every illusion. I need you to be able to look clearly at this Earth plane reality fearlessly, to meet those experiencing it at the level they can comprehend, and *speak the truth.* Those three words are the magic key. You must never be silent. *You must never be accommodating of fear or the false reality. Yet you must speak the truth with My gentle Love and compassion always. Thus you will be heard.*

Thine eye must be single. Thus your reality is the truth. Then in everything you see you will see the truth— ***the truth that there are no victims, no perpetrators, only the illusion of no Love,*** the illusion that something else is happening, something that is yours to reclaim for Me.

If you slip down into the illusion, you begin to believe it's true. That is where the danger lies! Because you are co-creators. ***What you believe is what will come to be.*** Can you even imagine the joy of those who seek to continue the lie, the forces of anti-Love and anti-life when one of you succumbs to fear? It is the greatest prize! They have just captured their very own fully operational darkness generator, if they have captured you in fear! As you can imagine, the majority of those who are caught up in fear are lower vibration. Thus their creative impact is not very powerful. But one of you, a LightWorker—that is excitement indeed!

I reach out now to lift you—to lift you so close to Me that you do see as I see, love as I love. From here we shall pour and pour and pour the light. We shall call every heart, for the power of My Love is embodied in everyone. So even if they resist it, when My call comes, every heart does respond. This, too, is a law. The being may then choose again to cover himself and shut out the light— but some of it got in. So what I am telling you here is that in My name, with My Love, all of My Creation will respond. Dear ones, rejoice, for we can create our own cracks!

It is ONLY the cracked open heart that can grow. I have said many times that I have come to crack open hearts that they become large enough to contain Me. I have explained that this is law—from seeds in the ground to hearts in the world. I will come to crack you open. You are My seed, given forth to take root and grow. Even those who have chosen darkness—I crack their hearts, too. I crack them open because I love them and because I have made All

That Is. Thus, All That Is will respond to the law of transformation.

So here is what you, My beautiful LightWorkers, must know. *You are My agents here in the world. If your eye is single, if you are aligned with both My Love and My power (which is the power of My Love), you can reach out and crack open the recalcitrant hearts in My name.* In my single light, the one truth. But you cannot do this if you believe the illusion. You cannot possibly do this if you have any fear. You cannot do this if any part of you believes in the false reality. If you do, you will sink into the illusion with them, and then they can use you to fuel their reality. This is very, very important information. I ask you to really study this until you have mastered it. Of course I will assist you.

Even with those whom you love, especially as you grow in light quotient or power or amperage, if you agree with them in any way (and they are in an illusion), you have just made that illusion stronger. With every dedication of your life to Me you are more plugged in to My creative current. It becomes your energy with which to create. The closer we are, the more power is pouring through you, the more critical it becomes for you to be absolutely aligned with Me at the highest level, the level of the truth of Love.

You cannot ignore what is around you. You would be unable to relate to those you are meant to serve. Rather you must always be looking back on this "reality" from the level of truth, speaking what that truth reveals through you every moment. This is My promise to you. If you place your eyes solely on Me, if you reach up until you can experience the truth of Love, I will always pour the true vision of each situation, so you can create the crack. So you can invoke My promise that I will pour the truth, the single light of truth, to you.

There are none in all Creation who cannot be reached. It is simply that to reach them you must have as much energy invested in truth as they have in deception. If you can hold the truth, unwavering in the face of that anti-Love energy, it will shake them. It will shake the energy of duality which is brittle, for it is built of linear energy, abrupt and ungiving. It is actually easily shaken.

The main "weapon" that is used by those promoting separation—you know, of course—is fear. The teaching I am bringing to you is about conquering this. I will not use the word transforming, because it does not apply. In truth, the moment there is a crack in darkness the light makes it disappear. It does not need to be transformed. *It ceases to exist!* The strength of the darkness is in its illusion of strength. This does not mean that on this level of subjective reality it is harmless, for it certainly is not. But the truth is that darkness is not real. It is fear that keeps you from discovering this.

So here we are. My LightWorkers are gathering in a world of duality and a world in metamorphosis. I ask you now to create here in yourselves an oasis of truth. This light of truth is already carried forth in these words. The last great test. If you remember, it was Jesus' test, too. You must come to look in the eye of fear and know that it is not true.

Fear is the enemy—not "powers and principalities," not Lucifer and his minions. Fear is the only way they can have access to your hearts, My beloved humanity. Fear is the opposite of Love, just as darkness is the opposite of light. Without fear your hearts are made of Love. That is the truth, for your hearts are Mine.

A heart that knows its truth is invulnerable because darkness cannot crack open a heart. This was to be your protection as I allowed Free Will to be. Everything else that would seem to call darkness unto itself—avarice, hatred, any of it is always the result of fear. Always.

There are, truly, only two things at play. Naming them will give you strength. They are fear and Love. Love makes available the access to My light, for Love and light are two parts of one thing. Love is. Light is Love in movement.

So I charge you with the example. I charge you with the revelation. ***The truth, and the victory, is not in ignoring the darkness nor is it in fighting the darkness. The truth is in loving the darkness.***

You have heard it said that I love Hitler, which is your symbol for that which is most evil in the world. It is true. When I look upon that being My heart swells with Love. For I know all of you as Mine. And, should you feel yourself appalled that I would love such a person, I now remind you. There are no degrees. Love is Love. Darkness is darkness. Certainly you want Me to love you and whatever you have within you that believes in the lie. Thus, if you are to know Me, you must know that I have no degrees of Love. I love each and every one of you completely. Totally. Passionately. Tenderly. 100%. All you have to do is pull up the shade of fear and let My Love in.

So this, too, I place in your hands. The gift of My Love and its abundance. Once you have released fear you will finally be ready to accept all the good that comes from My Love. When you allow My Love in, its presence within you draws to you the response to Love—in everything, in everyone in your life, and in the full manifestation of your SoulMate. Then, once your Soul Mate is with you, you have the mirror in which to see yourself, to check yourself and to see how you are progressing in opening up to Love.

Remember, if there is not fear, there is Love. So *if there is ever any part of someone's life not perfect, you will find fear to be behind it.* Many times you will find fear in the way of people being able to even acknowledge a SoulMate or even the possibility thereof. You must all be fear-free. You must be alive only in Me.

There is no way yet to show you the immense joy you will have when you can truly walk into the illusion from the perspective of the truth, reach out your hand and lead My children out to freedom. I ask you never to believe in the power of darkness again but rather to see it all from My view. I will lift you up to see it, again and again, until this view becomes your reality for I tell you that even the most subtle fear is handing your heart to the anti-Christ.

Trust Me. Trust that you are Mine. Trust that I will protect you always unless you invite the darkness in. I ask you to give your allegiance to the single eye of light—the place from which I see everything. This may not be easy. Yes, this does have to do with belief. You are surprised I have said this rather than telling you it is as simple as believing it. I know it is not. You have faced the darkness, all of you. But this is so you will be better witnesses to the light.

I have asked you before to be ruthlessly honest, to be unbelievably perceptive, to be willing to see everything, including (especially) what is hiding in you. First you have to see it before you can eliminate it. Once you see your fear, and you name it and stand against it, then you can hold it up for Archangel Michael and the beings of light to take away. So this is the plan. It is hearts cleaned of fear through great honesty, becoming vehicles for the "spotlight of Love" to shine through.

Remember what I have told you and be ready for Me

to show you how to love humanity as I do—how to see the illusion they are playing in, while being fully present with Me. And (again, pay attention) since everything is a hologram, you can reach in and "crack open" the heart of the whole illusion, allowing the light entry.

From the level of truth, Love eliminates darkness easily. It is only the fear that has been carefully instilled that makes it seem any other way. Are you ready to give up your fear? You have done many other great and courageous things. This is next. This is another cliff for you to jump off of. You will all help each other as you keep refining your fearlessness for it must be cleared out of every corner of your life. Your ego will try to hide your fear from you, because lack of fear is perfect Love and perfect Love has no ego. So you will have need of your ruthless honesty. You'll have need of My light to reveal things to you and to bring forth the gift of the Love in every situation. It's always there. A lesson learned if nothing else. You can believe that every fear is covering over a hidden strength. You might find, as you look at your history, that there were those in your life who took great pains and went to great lengths to instill fear in you. See it, bless it, and thus be free.

It is an exciting time as humanity comes upon the opportunity to release the shackles of perceived limitation and to open up to their Love. The end of the lie is in sight. Help Me spread the word!

IF THINE EYE BE SINGLE

*Every single person
with whom you have even remote contact
is here for you to bless.*

The Power of Our Steadfast Gaze on God

I am here. I am always guiding each and every one of you. Yet you can only see Me based on the level of your vibration and your awareness. This is a very important understanding. I have often explained that all messages at this level of reality include the interpretation of the messenger. Including this one.

Yes, you do know this. Understanding this you will understand many very important things. You will understand that "incorrect" information DOES have an element of truth almost always, for *I am always seeking entry into every life.* I will always take "whatever I can get," as you say. I will rush into every crack. I will flow through every heart, even if I am sharing it with ego, because at least I am there. I have a "foothold" in that person's life. So when a person says they are working for Me, they are. But what is received is filtered through their ego and therefore is brought forth as a mixed message. This is why you must all strive continually to lift yourselves up in Me. This is why you must seek to be only the clear vessel for My Love.

This can be very confusing at times. For someone who is not aware of the ego at work in their lives, you can see how they would long for the success of Love and the peace (true peace) that comes through Me. Yet it would be evading them.

Dearest ones, you must "live your truth." *You must*

live your truth SO deeply, so profoundly, that you will immediately know if anything in your experience is NOT your highest truth. In this, you will know your own energy, your own relationships, your own connection with Me so perfectly that the moment the energy changes, you will know it. You can recognize your own energy. You can recognize your light. You recognize the vibrational pattern that is you at the highest level. Then you will be able to always attune yourself to that level.

Now let us talk about the deepest truth—your relationship with Me. Dear ones, I want you to see how it is for others. I want you to know how it is to be challenged to discern—to find out how subtle are the nuances of the world. *I want you to cherish every effort made by any human being, no matter how small it may seem to you.* Though you may have literally been through hell on Earth, most of you have always had an inner conviction. Even before you could recognize it, it was operative in your life. So most of you have not ever known how it felt to be totally lost. *So what I want you to learn is tender Love and the deepest compassion for those who are struggling to choose Me. I want you to grasp deeply with your whole heart how carefully you will need to "shepherd" your brothers and sisters to me.*

Oh My beloved ones, how you must love them! How you must cherish every attempt to make contact with Me! How you must gently assist others, starting with those closest to you and moving outward. When you do this, we will be able to gently and so lovingly lift them up and deliver them into the perspective of the true self.

To do this, you must stay so close to Me that there is no separation. No distance at all. So close that your heartbeat and Mine are the same, that your whole being rests completely open in Me, facing upward, heart opened into

Mine. Feel the communion of Love until the Love pours forth, overflowing the cup of your being and filling each and every heart that is near you. When you do this, when the Love overflows from within you, every single heart that comes into contact with you will have its truth revealed.

Please pay attention. As we touch each heart together, dear ones, you will see the hearts crack open before you. You will experience My Love reaching through you to touch others. This is a great honor. As these hearts open before you, they will be very vulnerable. They will be holding out their pain for you and for Me. They will be offering their deepest selves up for healing. You must be very careful. *You must be very careful to honor what is happening.* You must love them as I love them and completely allow Me to love them through you. Their hearts will open further. You will be the bearer of My healing Love. You must love them as I love them. And as you do, miracles will occur. Hearts will be healed.

What I am saying here is this. *You must understand SO deeply, with such compassion what is happening that by the power of your steadfast gaze on Me, you NEVER WAVER. You are NEVER "fooled" again into believing anything other than perfect Love.* You also must understand that everything (everything!) is vibration. Everything is related to the "quotient of light." I can be pouring my Love through you to someone but if you are looking at the person's breaking heart (as it cracks open right before you in the light), and if your human self makes the interpretation of My message, it will be a message at a lower vibration. Keep lifting yourself, dear ones. Keep lifting to let Me take you. Let Me hold you in My Love. *Know that only Love is real.* In My Love, all is perfect, and at any moment, My Love can come in and "switch the channel" to bring in beauty and perfection.

So here it is again (and again and again), the full picture of what My LightWorkers are accomplishing. Because you will remain connected to all levels of human life, every human being who touches your energy and the energy of this work will find a connection. They will recognize that they are recognized. They will feel My Love directly because it can and does move right through you to them on their "wavelength." Being so recognized will crack open their heart. Right there before you.

You all must recognize what an honor this is. Yes, you will see the places they are the most hurt and you will love them for Me. You will love them AS Me. You will love them as Love itself which is what you are. You are living Love. As you love them for Me, I will be "brought down" through you so that person will experience Me through you. To do this, to be this, dear ones, you will need to know the great truth of what is happening, of what can be accomplished. As they connect with Me through you, they will be transformed. Their heart will be healed. They will be "made ready" for their SoulMate and for their part in the awakening.

So you see, if you were to view this as their "neediness," then you will be confronted with tons of it! And you would not be able to do your work. Can you see? Can you see how clear you must be? My beloved ones, this is the same as if you were standing in an operating room, literally holding someone's heart in your hands! You will be holding the essence, the heart of their being, in front of you. You will need the greatest tenderness, the greatest clarity and the greatest ability to heal them, to "do the transplant." So they "go in" an ego centered being. They "come out" a heart centered being, ready to manifest their SoulMate.

ALLOW NO JUDGMENT. Please. For if you allow judgment as someone opens his/her heart to you, you create an opening for the anti-Christ. The anti-Love energy. What is given in sacred trust must be honored. The statement of your being, every bit of it, is an invitation to every human being to open their heart.

Dear ones, you know, of course, how I love you—how very great a part you are to play. You must also know that you all must have the very greatest Love and integrity. *Where your attention goes, your energy follows.* The answer is understanding and then, of course, choice. I want you to see all the subtleties of how energies work in human life. I want you also to see that they can all affect you. Thus you will have a "healthy respect" and your ego will not be able to pretend to you that you are invulnerable and therefore you can judge those who succumb.

So you see, again, that you must courageously see and name all that is occurring while remaining high "above," up on the vibrational scale, that you may serve Me, serve Love perfectly. You must be ready to serve the light as the Great Shift takes place.

No matter whether
you are expanding through the cosmos
or focusing ever deeper inward
to the microcosm,
you will see that Love
has no beginning and no end,
and neither do you.

Seeing the Physical Self
from the View of Our Spirit.
The Shift in Consciousness

A vast magnificent light is who you are. A grand being whose golden aura pours out over the countryside— this is who you are. A heart with divine Love pouring through it —this is who you are. When, at last, you understand, you will see the vastness of your being and you will see that "way down there" like a little speck at the bottom of the movie screen, is your body.

This, dear ones, is what I want you to understand. This is the shift in which you grasp the truth of consciousness. This is the shift in which you understand the difference between the background and the foreground of your lives. It is to all My beautiful LightWorkers that I give this message. You must make the shift into living in your real consciousness—not from the body "looking up" to Me! No! Rather, it is time for you to live in your expanded consciousness, "looking down" on your body.

Dear ones, it is when you are awake to the great expanse that you are in communion with all life. It is when you are aware of your expanded consciousness that you can reach out and find the true perspective in every situation. You can reach out your hand, and it will be taken by angels. You can reach out your Love and truly heal the world. It is when you are this vast and light-filled being that you can use this body's sacrifice in honor and in perfect, clear intent, and only from this perspective.

I ask you, please, to no longer pray to Me from within your human lives, all of you. Rather, reach forth to take My hand and to lift your consciousness to who you really are. That is the shift of the true awakening. If you decide this, you will be assisted in every possible way, for in this you find the Holy Grail. Here lies the key in the lock to your ascension. Not in the traditional sense. *Rather the ascension in consciousness is done with so much Love that you lift the world with you, perfectly.*

You are a vast and glorious being! You are like the rising sun pouring your warming and life-giving rays upon our beloved humanity. *You are not this body. It is your anchor in the world. It is the "peephole" through which such a cosmic being as you may look to see the "goings on" of humanity.* Thus it is your gift, but not your master.

These are not your eyes! (These physical eyes.) Not your eyes with which to see the truth anyway. Do not use them to give you information about reality. This small organ beating in your chest? It is one cell in your true heart! Thus, you must not judge the size of any part of you. Nor can you use any of these senses, any of these "hungers" of the systems for obtaining information that is associated with this terribly limited point of view. If you do, you will be deceived. You will believe "the lie" that has been painted upon the canvas of the world by the limited vision of humanity.

These parameters are far too small for any of you. Please say "no" to being thus so limited. You are here, allowing the body consciousness to fill the whole screen of your view, all of you, and it is not. It is not the whole screen. In fact, it is a tiny speck. It is this that is the important thing you are to learn about consciousness. You control it.

Everything is now conspiring to "throw you out of orbit," to loosen you from your trajectory of belief, to pull you out of the gravity of your "humanness" and to help you fly free.

This is a huge shift. When you have made it, dear ones, then we are ready to bring people close to be warmed and washed in your light, for then you will be able to see the truth. Then you will know when someone is fooling you, and when there is a "leak" in someone's energy. *You will see their consciousness rather than their human reality.* If that is not the most exciting sentence you have ever read, trust Me that one day it will be.

You have a glimpse, all of you who seek the light, for you have been lifted—lifted in My Love, lifted in My presence. *You have had moments, each of you, where you made the shift, where you "slipped the bonds of Time and Space, reached out your hand and touched the face of God."*

It is time. It is time for Christ to come again. It is time for the light to become your reality. It is time to shift your reality completely. Every force of nature, every angel, every ascended Master, every being who serves the light is conspiring to force you through the gate. Each of you has had enough transcendent experiences to have a frame of reference. After you have accomplished this shift, you will be able to provide the frame of reference for others. I don't have to tell you how important this is. If everything is consciousness, people have to know how to recognize the experience.

A vast being, filled with the golden light, spreading out through the heavens, in communion with the angels, in awareness of the perfect unfoldment necessary for humanity, you breathe in the glorious expansiveness of your being. You acknowledge My presence. You joyfully rejoice in the Love pouring through your heart. *This pouring Love is the key because as it flows through you, it will draw to itself the truth of Love on every level of your life.* Thus, as you feel the Love pouring through your heart, you will glance down upon your physical vehicle, your body. You will feel such gratitude for the honor of its service. Your spirit will leap in joy and you will then observe the body in reverence.

You will see the light rising up in waves around your body. You will then see all the "cords" or openings connecting your body to the world. You will be aware, all of you, of the power of these connections and you will see the beings of light lovingly using these cords, each of a certain vibration, to connect you to someone or something needing Love. When the connection is made, you will immediately see Love and light being pulled through your body. Light will be poured in, and whirling with the vortex of energy, it will shoot out of the openings provided by your life to touch and heal and love and uplift. The most important thing, dear ones, is the shift in your consciousness.

All who are close to Christ, all who are living in the presence of My Love are being used in every possible way right now. Do not worry about your bodies, any of you. Do not worry, but make the shift now. This moment. And this moment. And the next.

Dear ones, there is a battle raging—a battle far bigger than the battlefields of any current war. You know that *I do not want you focused there.* But you also must know that I will always deliver to you the truth on every level, for it is only with such knowledge that you will know how to act. Only with such knowledge will you realize the scope of resolve necessary to bring this Earth and My children back fully to the light.

The best way that you can serve is to honor the crucible of God, which is all of you. It is crucial now to make the shift in consciousness for it is your Love, dear ones, that "does the burning," that transforms the "trash" into heat and light, that transforms hatred into Love and bigotry and separateness into the consciousness of unity that is the salvation of the world.

The perceptions that you have of a normal body having any kind of physical illness has nothing to do with your reality, any of you. *As a LightWorker, everything that you go through is carefully orchestrated.* It is always connected to the healing of the world, the upliftment of all life upon the Earth, the opening of human consciousness and the intensity of Love that it takes to make this shift.

What you are experiencing in your bodies is about the battle for the world that is raging. All who serve the light are trusting you to hold the line against the darkness. They are giving you the most critical tasks. You know this in your heart. And yet you can give these things no acknowledgement. None. Please! Essentially you are making this choice for humanity and by making it you are transmuting "the lie." Every time you do it. You must see only the light. You are re-living the question first asked. You are re-living the Garden of Eden. *Will you eat of the fruit of the tree of Good and Evil? Say "no," dear ones, for that was the moment humanity chose the lie, when one person, one SoulMate couple, chose to see other than Love, other than Me.*

So every time you are experiencing something through your body or through your life, remember who you are. Remember, oh, please remember the huge (what a lacking word!) importance of your choice. There must be no good and evil, dear ones, in order to heal the split in the world. There can be only good, for in truth that is all there is. You are each the crucible, thus in you the choices made by humanity are brought to you for review, for transformation. ***To transform is to see only good.***

Please listen. If you are living in your body consciousness, it is too hard to do. It can be so immediate, so real, so painful, so frightening, that it is too risky, so risky that you will not be able to discern the lie. My beloved ones, you cannot have a normal human consciousness in any way, including viewing life from inside your body looking out. It is time for the shift into your large consciousness.

At first it will still come in "experiences"—you'll have it and then you won't. But if you recognize the importance of those experiences and claim them as your full time reality, you will change swiftly. Dear ones, very soon, oh very soon, you must be in such beautiful communion with Me that when you do anything, I will be doing it through you. In this way can I "direct" my "army" of the light and inspire and uplift them, and directly shower them with blessings. In this way can you, in your expanded consciousness, work together with other LightWorkers to transform what needs to be transformed throughout the world.

Very importantly (could even be most importantly), when you have made this shift there will be no ego. ***If you —as your spirit — fill the entire screen of your consciousness, the ego will no longer exist.*** And it will be easy. You will know when you are there, ego free, because every one of you knows how it feels when I am moving through you. ***You know how it feels to be lifted and to be filled with light. That is how you will live your lives.***

This moment in history is PREGNANT with meaning, for the New World is about to be delivered. You have long known you are to be its midwives. The wait is over.

I have used many analogies and I have done so for a reason. Within these words are the "codes" that you will recognize telling you that your time has come. These are codes that were "implanted" within you to be activated when it was time to begin your work. It is time. So I ask you to trust that everything is right, as it should be, even if you are experiencing illness and distress of the body. Dear ones, this is transmutation. It is not only of yourselves, as you know, but I do promise you that you are a part of what is happening. It is not only that you are doing this for others. You are also burning out from within you the last residues of fear that block the embodiment, the incarnation of the Divine Feminine and the Divine Masculine.

Remember the fires that are spoken of in *Revelation?* Ah, yes, you do remember. These fires are within you. These are the fires of purification held within the beings of My starseed children, those who have ever loved Me. Remember how you offered to do anything necessary to bring the others back to Me? Because you knew the beauty of being close to Me.

It is the fires of transformation that are covering the Earth just as recorded in the Bible, only they are not visible to the physical eye but to the eye of the spirit. They do not burn the materials of wood and paper and the physical creations. They burn the "dross" of consciousness. This, dear ones, is why you must raise your vision to that level—the level "where the real action is." This is not the level of the battle of dark and light (contrary to much popular belief) but the level of pure Love. From this level will you be able to see truly. From this level you will be able to gaze down upon My children and to bring through Love, in every manner, through every little crack of an opening.

From this place of perfect Love you will be the steady choice for Love and by the nature of your being you will transform all energies less than Love through everything you do, in absolutely every way. The choices you make now are so critical. *Every thought makes the choice of what to do with humanity's energy running through you at that moment.* This realization will definitely solidify your commitment, and clarify the moment to moment choice.

Remember, I will tell you the truth of the many layers of consciousness and thus of realities untold (many many realities). But *your reality must always be Me. Attention on the light. You can acknowledge what is happening and then immediately take it to its highest reality, highest "translation" of which you are capable.* As you do this regularly, this will also greatly assist in making and maintaining the shift in consciousness I am asking of you.

This, dear ones, is to be the template of how you work with everyone. *You must have the greatest respect for each person's accomplishment, even if it is simply continuing to live in the middle of the illusion of fear and separation. Then, and only then, coming forth in PURE LOVE, DIVINE LOVE, will you ever offer your assistance in giving them another possibility.*

It is crucial now
to make the shift in consciousness
for it is your Love, dear ones,
that "does the burning,"
that transforms the "trash"
into heat and light,
that transforms hatred into Love,
and bigotry and separateness into
the consciousness of unity
that is the salvation of the world.

Teaching Transformation is Critical
December 2001

*E*very year at the Christmas Season, the hearts of humanity open wider than at any other time. Well, this year, dear ones, is a critical year. It is a year in which the light must begin to penetrate the illusion and, most especially, to penetrate human hearts.

I now show all of you how to consciously use the connection with your physical experiences to aid in transformation for the world. I explain to you how to use the "crucible" which is your body, to claim consciously your service to the world—how to awaken the connection of My transforming Love through all of your layers of your consciousness (stepping it down), and then through your body and out to humanity.

As you begin to do this work, many of you LightWorkers will finally accept who you are and what you have come to do. One of the greatest reasons you must understand this part is that *through this, the gift of transformation, you will give millions of people a path that will give meaning to their suffering, a way through their challenges.* It is only by giving that one receives. It is also true that *the process of transformation is the only way* (please let this sink in)—*the only way—that all of humanity can make this shift.*

In this plan there has come together the greatest thought and the greatest Love of all of the beings of light who guide and guard humanity. In this plan has been born the involvement of many beautiful humans who are on the

"Path." In the dedication of so many souls to humanity has come an unexpected and very great blessing—the engagement of the law of Love that will be the greatest source of advancement for the Lightworkers that has ever occurred.

Dear ones, as you read of My plan for the raising of your bodies into light, please rejoice. But also know that you will have this when the time is right. Now it is most important to understand the full teaching that is to be brought forth from any and all of your unhealed lives, using them for everything they are worth.

The entire world today is based on selfishness. It is the sole attitude that pervades almost everything. (There are rare exceptions in very remote areas, but even there it is coming.) Dear ones, if you were to go forth, as Jesus did, teaching that people are meant to raise up their bodies, very few (very, very few) people would understand.

At this juncture of the world, it is not appropriate for one person to be the focal point, as Jesus became. It is not appropriate at all, because now is the time of the raising of all humanity. It is time for people to turn within, to live the spiritual life. The greatest obstacle to this, the world over, is selfishness. The self-centeredness of the ego has been blown up by the cultures of consumption and independence. What has resulted is the terrible loneliness of complete separation assuaged by filling up with goods bought or food eaten or sexual encounters.

Many people have never truly given of themselves, ever. I am talking of the vast majority of humanity. Almost every Love relationship has always been orchestrated by the ego, whose focus is ever on getting. Oh dear ones, as you know, *we must give people back their soul, their true humanity. We must connect people to the circle of life so that giving, they then begin to receive.* As you know, it is the release of the gift that draws energy back in. Always.

Thus, now I will speak of your work—the work of your lives as transformers in the body. This work gives others a tangible option that will connect them to real life and grant them the gift of giving (and receiving). Secondly, as you experience these people, as you become more involved in this ministry of giving, you will understand the needs of humanity. Consequently, you will be able to use your own powers of transformation to raise up those who are in need. You will be able to connect with them and pour My Love through directly.

It is time for the fairy tale ending for humanity, but most have no idea where to find the story, let alone how to play their part. Should you doubt, glance through the weekly magazines or turn on the television.

There are many reasons you return again and again to the beautiful story of Jesus of Nazareth. But you are not meant to duplicate his ministry. He came to show the possibility of every human. You LightWorkers are here to show each one the path. That path is having the vision within each being of My Love and their perfection at all times. *Each human being must use his or her life and its events as an offering of Love for the transformation of humanity and the Earth into the New World. Now.*

The two parts of this path are very important, for dear ones, every person must, by choosing his or her thoughts, grow into his or her true potential. At the same time, people can also offer the precious energy released as they make a turn, as they change their minds. I have explained how so much is released when one person turns back to Me. If this energy is dedicated, given forth for My use, humankind will be leaping to their awakening.

The body is meant to be spiritualized as the heart is opened and consciousness is raised. This is true. But there is an awakening you have come to serve and the least of our problems is the raising up of bodies at present. *The urgent need is a path of awakening for humankind that will make sense to them and will take them quickly, all of them, into the vibration of the New World.* Once accomplished, the rest will be natural.

Dear ones, if you will remember, you came to Me with this plan, along with the other LightWorkers who saw the potential. *You saw the potential change that you could each bring about by personally taking on a river of darkness and stopping it in its track—transforming the energy and thus lifting up all who had been damaged by it.* There are many who have taken on a piece of this. However, many of these have fallen asleep. They have forgotten.

Beloved ones, when you examine the potential and the need, it is difficult to gauge which will offer more possibility—the reunion of SoulMates or the path of transformation. The need for both is very great. Each offers a great opportunity for the awakening of our beloved humanity. A SoulMate couple who becomes aware of their power of co-creation and turns it to the service of awakening, will change the world exponentially as the ripples go forth from their every dedication to the awakening. Yet it takes someone who is capable of saying "yes" to Love, of choosing their heart, to say "yes" to their SoulMate.

Thus far, there are many who still define their lives as difficult or challenging, and the awareness that they can use those challenges to bless and heal humanity will be more liberating, more uplifting than anything they could dream. And their blessing will truly be the greatest gift that anyone could ever give.

Every thought that has ever gone forth —
or in truth, is going forth in the eternal Now,
for Time is an illusion —
is alive in Me.
It has been created.
It is a reality.

The Blanket of Protection
As We Create the New World

*T*he world that is before you is a world of joy, a
world in which you are wrapped every moment in a
beautiful communion filled with golden light, supported
perfectly in a gentle union with those who share your world.
Opening your heart to Me in deepest trust, you will find
that you are floating through each day in complete
attunement. If you have one thought of need, you will
reach out your hand and the need will be filled. As you turn
your attention to your beloved SoulMate, you are flooded
with the ecstasy of each other's holy presence, lighting up
your heart and mind, lighting up your life so brightly that
you are becoming a living sun. You are a star of pulsing
light that is ever radiating Love to all who draw near.

The world that is before you is an experience of such
Love, of such deep communion that you are consciously
blessed by all life around you. The wind truly sings to you
of glory, and you are wrapped in the bliss of knowing and
being known, heart-to-heart, consciousness-to-consciousness.

The world before you is composed of great trust. It is
a trust deeper than any human feeling. Trust that is
unshakable in its presence. Trust that lifts and colors every
moment of your life. Trust that I am always here, supplying
you with grace, caring for your every need, living through
your heart, as you live in Mine.

In this world there are no mistakes, no experiments
that can fail, no Love that is ever lost. Each and every step

you take will be guided perfectly by Me, and because you choose Love as your reality, you will be Home at last.

This world is closer than you think. It is close not only for the few of you who "know," but for the many who are still locked within the dream, who still struggle with a nightmare of lack, of greed, of anger and of hatred. I am cracking open your hearts—the hearts of all My children. Just as in a dream, it is at its most intense before you wake. I am shaking awake My children. As I shake, in those last minutes of sleep, the dream of life in the world of separation is engaging those who are still asleep.

What of those already awake? Ah, it is to you that I am reaching now, for you have come to see that Love is the only truth. You have made the choice to love and to release all else. Thus, for you, the dream is fading. You are the awakening SoulMates.

As surely as Love is your true reality, Love is also your personal experience. When you awake and open your heart, Love is all you see. So from the shadows of the dream will come the birth of Love that is your SoulMate, that is your physical environment, that is your experience of Nature, of your animals, of your livelihood. Of everything.

Before, I called you lucid dreamers—those who could remember you were caught in a dream. Now, I call you awakening ones, for the dream is rolling off of you and the clear light of truth illuminates your way.

Thus, when you find Love all around you, when the experience of Love comes to speak to you in everything through the gentle language of the heart, I ask you to get ready. Get ready to assist in the greater awakening. If ever I needed you, I need you now. *I need you sharing in the preparation for the birth of humanity into the truth of*

their being. I need you ready, ready to be guided every moment, to be assisted into place. Ready to work as a team of light as never before experienced. Ready to become a part of the unified heart of humanity.

You will find your SoulMate. Open your heart and he or she will appear. Waste no time in yesterday. Do not compare this relationship, for nothing you have been before applies even vaguely to who you are today. Instead I ask that you join your hearts quickly, and as you blossom in Love, begin to create the shield of Love for humanity.

Years ago I brought forth the story of the awakening. Then it was a future. Now it is happening. In it I told that ***there would come a time when those who are awake must build a safety net of Love, to protect Creation at the time of the awakening.*** For those who have not heard this message, I bring you now a recap.

You are My children, oh beloved humanity. As such, you are pieces of My heart. Everything I am, you are. All that I create, you can create also.

There was a time frame to our agreement that you would come to gain the precious gift of individuality. This was a precious gift beyond your ability to comprehend, for only thus could you become strong enough not to dissolve back into Me. Thus, you came to take on this life of ego and separation to learn who you are and to be able to maintain "structural integrity" in My presence. You had to be able to resist the pull of this knowingness - the great Love that would bring you back into My heart - while maintaining your identity.

Unlike most who have conjectured an evolutionary path, I now bring you the truth. You have always held within you an understanding that you had a finite time to complete your growth, for just as I breathed you out into the world of form, so will I call you back into Me.

The time is here. In the next 12 years I am bringing you Home. Twelve years to you. To Me, the moment between breathing out and breathing in. Now you are ready. You are ready to have the parameters of your world be changed and ready to experience whatever it takes to shake you all awake from the dream.

You are co-creators. This you know, those who are reading this. I need your help, as you need Mine. Thus, as you give, you will receive. You will grow and spread open your heart, spread the wings of your unlimited thought, and you will rise. You will rise into the freedom and the truth of who you are.

My beloved ones whose hands are together on the doorknob in the doorway of your freedom, I remind you of the greatest truth of all that lives and has its being within Me. **You must give in order to receive. To know Love, you must give Love.**

As humanity is released from the protective womb of Time and Space, every thought will begin to manifest. As the density of the Earth vibration lifts, you will instantly know what lives within you every moment, for what lives within will manifest. Immediately. This is how Creation works. The light of Love pours into life, and especially into human beings. As it pours in, it is molded by belief, right then.

In the Old World, now leaving, there was an artificial barrier—Time. This barrier was your protection so that what you thought had a force pushing against it and thus could not immediately manifest. As you can imagine, just from imagining some of the potential thoughts of human beings, there were many nightmares lurking. Only by the repetition through Time would a person's thoughts fully manifest, although they were always a factor in everything.

Even now there is such small awareness that your thoughts are a creative force, aided by your emotional state. For some of you this will be a blessing to hear, but for others who are deeply asleep in the dream of separation, there is danger. There is danger to these beings that if the light pours in without the mediation of Time, their thoughts could destroy them.

And there is a greater danger, for which I now come to you for assistance. You are My children. You are all made to create. *Beloved ones, if the protective veil of Time and Space comes down, what will be created? Will the thoughts of darkness and separation that have plagued the protected Earth reality spread forth, introduced by you, My beloved children? They must not!* And yet, all of us, you and I alike, know that every human being must come Home, brought in Love back to the great truth I am, and thus the truth that you are also.

You must intervene. You must create the protection that will shelter My children as they awake. You, My beloved ones, My LightWorkers, those whose hearts are remembering, you must do this, for this has all been about your Free Will, about remembering who you are. So again, as the light of truth dawns, I send to you My greatest Love. I pour to you My greatest messages, wrapped up as angels, as children, and as SoulMates, dedicated to the awakening.

Thus I ask you to begin to pour forth the blanket of protection which is what I name the Divine Feminine. This is outgoing Love. Compassionate Love. Totally giving Love. Love in which there is no desire to receive in return.

This is a different kind of Love, for in truth, most Love will always be received back by the one who gave it forth. That is the nature of Love and of life. That which is given always returns. This is the truth of the SoulMate. You open your heart. You become Love, and Love will become everything you experience. *Except for the gift of the Divine Feminine.* This is the Love of the Mother, the nurturer, giver of Life. This is a part of Creation, a part of All That Is, of All I Am.

In Creation, as I have explained often, the movement became the Divine Masculine and Divine Feminine. In every SoulMate couple, whatever their bodies, there is a Divine Masculine and Divine Feminine embodied one in each person. Now, knowing this, it is time to understand these energies as forces of Creation, and as the blanket of Love (feminine) and the urge to action (masculine) that must be harnessed to transform the world.

There are many who know that the world is transforming, and that these are the last days of the dream, the illusion. It is time for Sacred Sexuality, but not only in the sense of the co-creative power inherent in the joining of two human beings (especially in true Love, as SoulMates). It is time for you to understand the very forces of Creation, forces that live within you. These forces are awakening in those whose hearts have opened. These forces are yours to direct. In fact, *these are forces that you must direct, for this is the planet of Free Will and you are the children of My heart.*

Thus I ask you now to begin the course of study that will bring you into intimate communion with the very forces of life. I ask you to know that these are yours to use with Love, in the service of the awakening of our beloved humankind. As you do this, as you open your being to a new experience and new expression, you can and must trust that, as your world changes as a result, everything in it will be there to support you. If it is not, it is because you yourself are blocking it. I promise you that *as you begin allowing Love to use you in Love's great divine capacity, it will draw to you the power of your greatest good, greater by far than anything you can dream.*

So here we are, standing on the cusp of the dissolution of Time. Here we are on the cusp of the world of this third dimension. Please, My beloved LightWorkers, hold this vision. *Hold this vision. Ask Me to assist if you do not receive it.* All who are wielding Love consciously are standing beyond the Earth, outside of Time and Space. You can see the stirring as the hearts are responding. You can also see the ego and all who have used it for selfish purposes as it seeks to keep My children sleeping.

Know this. *Everyone will awaken. It is not a question of who decides to choose the light. It is done, essentially, for all of you are Mine.* So where would you ever go but Home to Me? Yes, there are many layers of this, the majority of which your mind cannot comprehend. Suffice it to say that other than in the pocket of the Earth, Time does not exist. So once you have risen into Love, it will be clear to you that all of humanity is now going to awaken. It is written in the books of Heaven, the code of the DNA within you.

Yes, it may occur through some amount of Time here on Earth, but from your vantage point now, as you look down upon this awakening, what you will see is this. *I am calling and human hearts respond.* The force of this response begins interrupting the dream. For some, awakening is easy. For others, the dream may become a nightmare as that which is within them is exposed to the light. The more they are shaken, the more intense is the nightmare. They are dreaming that their world is falling apart. (It is.) They dream that all they believed is not true. (It isn't.) They may feel cornered in the dream, so they attack. And on it goes. Faster. More intense. Until at last the shaking finally wakes them. Startled, they look around. "It wasn't real!" they think. And for the first time, they can feel the relief—the relief of knowing that I am here, holding them. They know that they are loved beyond measure, that nothing they do can ever change this. The light then penetrates their being, pulsing through them.

This is the critical point. At this moment, they are not in the dream. They are not in the protective womb of Time. They are not in the "off phase" energy of Space. They are in Reality. And they are co-creators (this has never changed). ***Everything they think, everything they believe, they now create in Reality.*** In Creation. In All That Is. In Me. Therein lies the danger. Balanced on this point of awakening, they now fully form the light according to their beliefs.

It is for this moment that I come to you. It is for this moment that I ask you to create the shield of Love, made by human Will, fashioned from human Love, sent forth in the energy of the Divine Feminine—the greatest law of Given Love.

If the blanket of your Love protects them, if the great service of your Love, your gift of the Divine Feminine is then waiting, they will be wrapped in its protection. They will, in this moment, understand giving in the real sense. Giving as I have given of Myself, that all life is formed from My substance. Giving in a true experience that is beyond your current words to express. Giving as the tender opening, the pouring forth of all creation into each and every created life, into that person who awakens. They will understand through the blanket of that Love, of My Love as the great ray of nurturance, bringing forth giving of everything for the purpose only of giving, tenderly wrapping each person.

That person, awakening with receptiveness, in that moment, will understand. Understanding, they will greet Creation as living Love, as the God-self they are —as the receptacle of these great cosmic forces of masculine and feminine, and, by the gift of human Will, the director of true co-creation.

Moment after moment, awakening after awakening, there must be the gift of this great and tender Love waiting. It is waiting to offset the continuation of the dream. It is waiting to illuminate each human being—to show them, in that instant, the truth of Love so clearly that Creation is protected, and that Love is the only creation.

Yes, there are "fail-safes" that have to do with vibrational capacity, but even at a low level it is important not to contaminate the larger Creation. It is My plan, My only desire, to welcome you, My beautiful children, into your heritage of Love without further delay.

It is this shield of Love that the LightWorkers will create. This is the next step up from transformation. Right now, I have asked you to assist Me in transforming the energies of ego and anti-Love. Soon you will be leaving this behind, for transformation requires the acknowledgment of negativity. It continues to create a world in which darkness /shadow/anti-Love, is an acknowledged reality. This means you are lending it the power of your creative mind. This will work a little longer—and it will assist greatly. But then I will ask you for another leap in consciousness, dear ones. The leap you are taking everywhere. The leap into the embracing of the forces of Creation themselves—within you, as your SoulMates, and moving through the universe—waiting for you to command them.

Send forth the Divine Feminine now, to create this blanket of Love around the Earth on every level, through the Earth in every atom. Do this, that all that is not yet awakened will be lovingly embraced by the Mother force I Am, by the Love that I am giving, Love in which I do wrap each of you continually. You are co-creators with Me. Thus it is easy for you to say, "winds, come play," "angels, come protect me," and "forces of Creation, I send you forth."

This is not only for females to do. This is for human beings. It is for every child of Mine to come into direct contact with the living power of Love as it moves forth to create.

Dear ones, I am now pointing you directly into the coming experience of true human Sacred Sexuality, of the living embrace of Love as human beings. It is with these forces of Creation that you will find your answer. True Sacred Sexual Union is the joining of two cosmic beings uniting their entire beings, which are vast and glorious, in a complete union that creates one of the two. One heart, one desire—to Love. One Will—to give forth Love. And one result—the embodiment, on all levels of Creation, of the energies of the Divine Masculine and Divine Feminine.

Oh, My beloved ones, the difference between this and current sexuality will be hard for your current imagination to hold, but please attempt to! I have given you, My beloved humankind, the ability to become the "First Split"—the energies awakened in Me by My desire to create. In becoming those energies, through the union with your SoulMate, I give you the entirety of the power of Creation. *Dear ones, when you get to this point, you will be My equal.*

This is when you will be the mirror that I longed for; the companion in the vastness of All That Is. In this embodiment, you become a separate heart within My heart —and you create a universe around you.

So now, having taken you to the great immense truth of SoulMates, of the future of humankind, I bring you gently back to planet Earth. I ask you to tenderly love the gift of this womb, of the planet that is its physical structure. I ask you to raise her with you that she may know the gift of nurturing My children.

I also ask that you dedicate your every breath, your every thought to Love, that you may see its embodiment quickly as your SoulMates, in ever greater glory and clarity—that together you may dedicate yourselves to this work of Love before you.

Practice every moment. Practice the communion with the Divine Feminine. Invite the power of Divine Masculine. Give your all to this awakening in yourselves quickly, so you can be in place.

Are you ready? Are you reading this? Then the answer is "yes."

I am waiting to teach you, to show you your beauty, and to demonstrate, through your Love, the power of who you are.

I will not even mention the necessary freedom from the limitations of ego, for you will easily move beyond it. Open to Love more and more deeply. Allow the amazement as you experience the beauty. Trust that I will lead you gently and perfectly.

It is a time of miracles—the miracle of Love and the awakening of humanity. Thank you for being ready.

What you name something is what it is.
This is the "dominion" of stewardship
and the acknowledgment
of your place as My children.
So as you see
that "blade of change" in your life
or in the life of the world in many ways,
please name it truthfully –
the blessing of opening the seed
for the light.

Re-Naming the World

December 2001

There is light pouring down into the Earth and the hearts of humankind. This light is of such intensity and this Love is of such tender magnificence that never before has there been such an opportunity. Truly at this time of Christmas 2001, the world is awaiting the birth of Christ once more.

In every human heart a seed is planted, a seed which when exposed to the light becomes the home of the Christ within. This is the light that, rising in each and every human being, proclaims, "Behold, a son or daughter of God!"

In all the world and in every heart there is a seed. It is a seed of the truth of this heritage of light, the heritage as My children. Sons and daughters of Love. Pieces of My own heart. And now the time is here. This is the time in which I come to crack open the seed, to pour in the light and to bring forth the new being that grows from this seed.

Dear humanity, a complacent seed is one that does not grow, for it exerts no energy in turning toward the light. A seed that cannot crack open can never become the potential within, for always and ever, the old must crack in order to expand to allow the new to come in.

So I tell you as I hear your prayers of confusion and concern over things that are happening in the world: it is only the sharp edge of change you are feeling. Do not fear. I have come to crack you open that I might come in.

I ask you now, My precious children, to believe in Me, your loving God. Believe that I have planted My Love so purposefully within. Believe that I have always known that there was a season for your opening, just as there is for any seed. Believe that what is planted within you is the heart within your chest—the heart that, cracking open, can see only Love. And in seeing only Love, you reclaim your heritage as Love made manifest in the world.

We come to another Christmas. Christmas is the time when all the Love that is in the world reaches upward, longing to be free, to recognize its bearer as My loving heart and to know itself in all it sees.

Dear ones, what this means is that you are Mine. You live and move and have your being in the sea of Love that is My being. Everything that is happening in the world around you now is meant to bring forth this opening. If you are not complacent, you are ready. If you are reaching farther than the normal answers, if you are beginning to see yourself in the faces of humankind helping one another, you are ready. You are ready for the sunlight of My Love, the gentle touch of Christ to take advantage of the crack in you, in the seed of your heart. In the seed of your beliefs.

Nothing will ever be the same. It is the end of this world as you currently define it. It is the birth of the world of Love. This moment. Starting here, in your heart. Everything that is happening is Love's to claim, Love's to transform, Love's to use to bring forth the Age of Peace.

What this means, My beloved precious humanity, is that every negativity can be seen for what it is—the blade that cuts open the seed to allow the New World to grow and bloom. All negativity can (and must) be claimed for this purpose. Every one. For you are Mine and you have dominion—dominion in both your inner world and in your world without.

Thus, **WHAT YOU NAME SOMETHING IS WHAT IT IS.** This is the "dominion" of stewardship and the acknowledgment of your place as My children. *So as you see that "blade of change" in your life or in the life of the world in many ways, please name it truthfully—the blessing of opening the seed for the light.*

Dear ones, only that which can cause you to think a new way can open you. Only that which can radically change how you see the world and how you see yourself can be enough. Enough to shake you awake. Enough to crack open all the layers of protection you have woven around your heart. Enough to crack open the deep shell of habit that holds you in one place, in one shape, in one relationship to Me, to yourself, to Love, to your life. Only then can you be ready.

All the events that have recently occurred are exactly for this purpose. To keep you awake! To make you appreciate life, to assist you to see in the mirror of world events how you may have been sleeping in the midst of the greatest time of humankind. September 11th was just such an event.

Now in saying this to you, I do not tell you that these things were caused by beings of light. They were not. But they are, absolutely, the result of the intensifying light, the advent of Love. By their nature both light and Love will reveal what is held in darkness, as a light turned on shows what is in the room. Such light will break up old calcified structures that are resistant to Love. More importantly, My beloved children, *you must know that what you see and speak and believe about these things is the most important of all.*

This is where I come to the blessing of Christ, of

Jesus, who held forth the perfection that is waiting for humanity. He will show you how to use these things. He will show you how to take that which is born of negativity and transform it into a living statement of the freeing power of Love. He will show you that *how you choose to see each thing, how you think of it, speak of it, and what you name it is everything.* And how every part of every experience is a pathway to transcendence, transformation, to reclaiming your heritage as My Love in embodiment.

Dear ones, Christmas is a time when the whole Earth and every being upon it is held with personal tenderness in the radiant Love of Christ. It does not matter what religion you are. It does not matter what you believe, because *Christ is simply My Love in a form close enough to reach you as you live in this world.* This is always true, the reaching forth of My Love for you and its gentle knocking on the "door" of your heart and consciousness.

This year is different. Why? Because I want you back. It is time for you to remember that you too are Christ. Christ is simply My perfect Love made manifest. It is born perfectly in your hearts. All you have to do is allow it. *All you must do is remember that Love is truly all that is.* That Love is you. My children, cells of My very heart! As soon as you say "yes," even to considering this, all that is not Love begins to crumble. To move. To open to reveal the kernel of Love that is you and thus, to anchor My heart in the world.

Rejoice in the truth of the seeming negativity in the world as Love's awakening. See that Love cracks open all that is old, rigid, all that seeks to keep Love restricted. *Know that as the light reveals all that was held in darkness, your Love can then set it free.* Christ can come to show the truth that was locked within the darkness.

Most often, beloved ones, darkness is simply fear that is wrapped around the Love. If you look with your heart, you will begin to see this. Those who have decided that Love is too dangerous, build walls to contain it, to "keep themselves safe." But since Love is your nature, being My children, it takes thicker and thicker walls and more and more energy to keep it away. Thus is such a person's life force consumed in protecting them from a false fear of Love, a fear that, when released, will bring miracles as well as relief.

There is so much that you do not know about Love! For you have been lied to on every side by those who stood to gain from your forgetting who you are. Not the least of these is your own ego. The return of Love means a life that is complete, filled with unity, complete with your SoulMate, drawing to you joy and peace but most of all unity. Thus the ego, whose purpose of individualizing you is ending, is truly fighting for its life.

Choose Love, dear ones. Choose Love. In every moment. *As the heart becomes the instrument through which you live your life, I promise you will be immersed in joy regardless of what is happening in the world.* And as you choose to see Love, so do you also create Love and thus, in every moment you also free the world.

Everything that is happening is to crack open the hearts of My children. Everything in each stage, personal and global, is the result of the incoming light. Does it meet resistance? Then it will be a bumpy ride. Bumpy as the obstacles to Love, once hidden, are revealed.

Yet once seen, you can change these obstacles, truly, through your consciousness, by taking My hand, placing your trust in Love, blessing them and turning your powerful attention to the light. For you are My children; thus you co-create through the power of your consciousness. *It is in "naming" that you create the world. In giving definitions to those things that you encounter. NAME THEM LOVE, EVERY ONE. Name the rough spots the awakening to Love and then breathlessly await Love's appearance from the ashes just like the rising Phoenix,* out of the ashes of your old belief, belief in darkness, in fear and most of all, in the power of Love to hurt you. I crack open your heart that you can emerge as Love.

I want to tell you again about the power of your attention, as you remember who you are. WHATEVER YOU PLACE ATTENTION ON, YOU CREATE. For you are My progeny. This is your world. Remember? Thus do you have "dominion" over the Earth. Dominion means that *AS YOU NAME IT, SO IT IS.* So far you have named it many things but you have not recognized yourselves so you could not be expected to recognize that the truth of life is Love. Now you are remembering.

As you remember, you will "rename" everything in your world. You will know all things as Love and thus will you draw into existence the truth of all life at last!

Recognize Love and it will reflect to you everywhere. Know yourself as Mine and the Love you are will always acknowledge the Love present everywhere else. Choose truth as your only reality and Love will come at last to stand before you as your SoulMate; to surround you as your "work," your service to the world; to greet you from within Nature; and to emerge in every situation that comes into your life, for at last you will recognize who you are.

Dear ones, Christ is the name of My Love, moving forth into the world. Thus does Christ return, to be embodied in you as you recognize yourselves.

It is still early in the Homecoming of the World, yet the seeds of Love are bursting open rapidly. The world you know is passing as the world of Love now manifests. Say "Yes" to Love! Say "Yes!"

I send you forth
with the very keys to the human heart
and to humanity's awakening.
This takes deep commitment, dear ones,
and it does take humility.
You must ever be serving
My Will.
If ever any of you believe that
you do the work in any way,
then you will become
a detriment.

Launching Ourselves Beyond the Pull of Self-Centeredness

I am reaching for you every bit as much as you are reaching for Me. It seems as though you must continually reach upward, that you must put forth the effort required before you can truly feel the grace of My Love. It seems that you must open your heart, your mind and your consciousness to be lifted into this light. But it is really not true. It is only that you have not learned to recognize Me in everything—so this is a pathway to your recognition. This is you, teaching your mind to allow Me in. This is you, opening your consciousness to the glorious truth of Love. ***In truth I am everywhere and in everything. In truth I am never separate from you.***

In the vibrating center of Creation, there is you! You, who are My heart, for My heart is truly the central point of absolutely Everything That Is. Thus, dear ones, no matter which way you look, you will always see Me. You will see Me and you will know Love, for Love – all Love in all Creation radiates outward through you.

Please take a moment to understand this. Even in your physical reality, if you feel Love, it originates in your heart. Then it moves outward to illuminate your consciousness, and to send signals to your glands releasing hormones to your body. In other words, what happens within you, once you can understand, is the same thing that happens in the larger universe. Ultimately, once you see with true vision, once you can understand the language of Love, you will be able to know Me by knowing yourself.

Just as you can know yourself by knowing Me.

Dear ones, all Love in Creation moves through you, for you are My heart. I ask you to take this in. Allow this awareness to fill you, to penetrate your consciousness, to lift and carry you into greater understanding. The understanding is that Love is your "work" in the universe. If you are My heart, then *everything and anything to do with Love is yours to attend to.* You are to direct Love as it moves through you. You are to assist Love to move unimpeded. And by following the Love that is pouring through you, you become acquainted with absolutely everything. The Love that flows through My heart is the Love that is Creation. My heart encompasses Everything There Is.

There will come a time when you will understand this. You will understand the truth of what you are and you will understand your vastness. You will understand that no matter which way you turn your consciousness, you will be looking at Love. *No matter whether you are expanding through the cosmos or focusing ever deeper inward to the microcosm, you will see that Love has no beginning and no end, and neither do you.*

If you are My beloved children, the heart of God, My heart (and I assure you that you are), then the nature of your being is as a container, a conduit of Love. The purpose of your existence is giving Love. Yes, I have already explained this to you, but I must show you, in every way I can, how important it is for you to recognize your real nature, and to understand your deepest spiritual purpose. Beloved ones, this will ultimately make sense out of everything in your lives.

The only energy that you must exert, dear ones, is to get out of this 'pocket' of reversed energy—to get enough momentum to get the reversed energy, the upside down reflection to flip. You will be instantly propelled forth into the truth of Love, into the true nature of your beings. You will come into a new relationship with life in which absolutely everything serves the upliftment of your being.

Dear ones, when you are free of this illusion, when you are back in your rightful position, you are in place in the universe. Your hearts are wide open in greatest joy, looking always toward Me as I pour the great Love I am through you to bless Creation. In position, oh dear ones, there is such great rejoicing! You will be feeling My Love pouring passionately through you, singing praise every moment to the great glory of Love, as you open and open and give yourselves over completely to the amazing experience of Love.

Together with your SoulMate you are an opening through which My Love pours every single moment. There is never a moment when you are not Love in movement, when you are less than the vehicle of My passionate, joyous, ecstatic gratitude at the gift of My glorious relationship. Every moment I am alive in the joy of the experience of Creation and the great gift of the opportunity to give Love. Through you I accomplish this, nourishing all that has come forth into existence as a result of My Love awakened and directed by My Will.

As My Love pours forth through My heart (the cells of which you are), every single thing I have created sings its joy in receiving the life-giving substance of Love – the substance of which all things are made. So when you are awake, dear ones, when you are completely open, freed of the reversal of giving into getting, every single moment is the complete communion of consciousness and heart with All That I Am. Once you are in alignment with all the energy of Creation, when you are "moving in the right direction," you are the suppliers of Love. You are forever giving, alive in the complete and total experience of Love.

It is, as usual, almost impossible to fully express this reality to you while you are here in this pocket of "reversed polarity"—for lack of a better way to put it. Once you are freed of the pull of anti-Love, your glorious experience of your true Reality will be effortless. I will explain to you the nature of the substance of Love and just how powerful a position you hold and how sacred.

My beloved humanity, I need you! I need you back in place! I need the cells of My heart to all be capable of pouring through Love. If you are not capable, then a part of Creation will suffer for it. Why? Because it is time. We knew when we began this that My body (which is Everything That Is in movement) could only be without the "life blood" of Love for so long before "damage" would occur. We also knew that you and I had to have each other to love, adore and relate to, so it was worth the risk for the great reward. The reward was your completely independent consciousness so that I could love you, so I could be surprised by you, and so that Creation could be expanded.

So we have always had a timetable. So many possibilities have awaited us. Now we are ready. It is time. And it is important. For as well as the great surprises you can create, you are needed to nourish, to uplift, and to give.

To be safe so that none of Creation would suffer, should your growth take unexpected turns (which it has!), there have always been those who have awakened quickly. These beings were nourished so that there would be a set of "older siblings" who could "hold the torch" and keep the Love flowing. As time has continued, this sacred team has increased in number and in dedication and awareness, so life will always be given Love and so you will always have caring hands reaching forth to teach you. These are what you have called the Ascended Host. They are holding stable the great opening of Love that is My heart that life can always and forever be grown and nourished and, thus, kept moving.

So we speak of giving Love for it is the nature of your being. It is the great truth of humankind. And, the reversal of this flow is the illusion you are caught in — the illusion that life can stop. ***The focus of humankind on Getting instead of Giving is the only real cause of death.*** Life is ever moving outward, for I am creating through the desire for relationship which is ever in movement. Getting draws in rather than giving out. Getting takes away Love rather than giving forth Love. Thus movement stops and death occurs. This is a very simplified version but you will find as you grow in understanding that it is accurate.

Dear ones, once you understand that the great effort that you must make to awaken your consciousness and to join with Love is temporary, you will be amazed at the difference this will make. Right now it is believed by many of My beloved children that there is an eternal battle between good and evil, that the effort needed to resist the self-centeredness must be exerted forever. The belief is that one little slip (or one big one!) and this energy of darkness will gain the upper hand. ***Now I can deliver to you, at last, the great truth that you are simply caught in a "Love Warp," a pocket of anti-Love and selfishness.*** You have been "engaged in a battle"–but a battle with an energy of anti-Love built up by your creating power used solely for the benefit of your "little selves." It is very much like Earth's gravity. Anti-Love is heavy and it makes you heavy. So in order to escape it, you will have to have a power source.

Just as a rocket has great propulsion systems that essentially create a contained and directed explosion of energy that breaks through the pull of gravity—so must you now develop a way to break free. You must get your selves out of the pull of getting, of wanting, of ego, and of self-centeredness. The most powerful, and easiest, method for doing this? Yes, you have guessed it! The Love of your SoulMate.

Dear ones, you can't even conceive the great power of SoulMate Love. I will tell you this. It can create anything you can dream of. It can easily free you from the confines of selfishness. SoulMate Love can free you from the lie of the illusion, the "false idol" of selfishness. I tell you that true Love can change everything. And it must! The time of anti-Love must end. *Dear ones, you are living against your true nature. Your entire world, especially the commercial or "developed" cultures has become completely corrupted by the constricting lie.*

I will not dwell on the terrible consequences of an entire planet ever more filled with the focus on everything you are not, but it is a far cry from our image when we began. *Yet completely intact is our connection. Completely intact is the truth of your being. Completely intact is My great Love for you. And completely intact is the truth of your being as Love.*

Dear ones, the "suction" of the reversal of the life force to getting instead of giving is very powerful. The beliefs and limitations keeping it in place are fostered diligently by those who, for various distorted reasons, believe they benefit. So it does take real determination to change the polarity of your thoughts and your heart. It takes all the decision you can muster, again and again.

Seeing how difficult this situation is and seeing how much force or power is needed to break through the pull of this "gravity" of reversal thinking and feeling, something became obvious to Me. *All beings of Love from all "corners of Creation" must now be enlisted to reunite the*

SoulMates. No other energy is so clearly attuned to Love, to the true nature of your being. No other possible path would switch humanity from getting to giving as would the SoulMate. This, too, will become ever more clear and obvious as you all grow in your SoulMate relationship.

Thus did My great desire for you, plus the timetable and the great need of life in the universe, call forth this intention in Me. Regardless of the density of matter and regardless of "unfinished karma" with other personalities, as of this time, this year [2002], a new dispensation is begun. *This dispensation, set in motion by My Love for you, is that your SoulMates can and will appear before you right away, as soon as you ask for them.* They will now be able to come forth through every avenue, especially being drawn ever more fully into the one who is now with you. SoulMates will be reaching forth into this reality from the higher dimensions to place more and more of their vital energy and consciousness here on Earth at this level of density.

Then will this teaching go out, alerting all of you to the necessity for the call to rise up within you continually for the fullest manifestation of your SoulMate possible in every moment, as your consciousness changes.

Then, My beloved humanity, I ask that you take hold of this great and powerful gift and give Love to your SoulMate unceasingly. Give, give, give, give! As you grasp the feeling of this Love, I ask you to allow it to "consume" you. Allow it to SING forth in every cell and every particle of your being. Love, Love, Love. And as you do, your vibration will accelerate and you will be "pointed in the right direction" because you are giving.

Then, ultimately, your energy will increase, fueled by your giving Love until you are launched back into your Home of eternal Love. From that moment you will be free.

Love will POUR through you absolutely effortlessly. You will know bliss. You will know who you are, what you are, and you will take your place together in the "higher dimensions." You will be an enlightened cell in My heart. Together, you will turn and bless humanity. You will become as the "Ascended Host."

Just like a rocket, you must be pointed in the right direction before lift-off. If you were not, it would be a disaster. (Just picture a rocket with engines igniting facing downward instead of up. "Not a good thing," as you say!) So your SoulMate relationship is My way of being sure that you will be going in the right direction when you start generating take-off energy. There are other ways of generating energy, of generating Love, but it is difficult to find anything else that can unleash the desire to give.

Even so, we cannot leave such important things to chance. So I will bring you back into deep contact with the steps and principles of choice for giving that are now so critical. Dear ones, knowing it is a short time now until you are free of "gravity," I ask for your full dedication to turning the direction or focus of everything in your life—especially your consciousness, and your heart.

There is no time to waste! Begin right away. Those of you who are with your SoulMate, those who have been growing into giving and to whom I have been teaching these principles, I ask you to begin to give forth in ever wider circles. Know without a shadow of a doubt that absolutely every person who comes into your life, whether for an hour or a day or ever enlarging contact, is there for you to give these blessings and an awareness of what is happening.

I am with you. Oh, beloved ones, say "yes" to Love. Your true nature is the giving of that Love.

*I am unfreezing your hearts,
My beloved children.
I am bringing Love as close to you
as it can safely get.
This I promise you.
There are no exceptions.
So all you have to do
is choose to gain control of thought
and to the degree that you accomplish this,
to that degree exactly,
will Love become your reality.
Closer and closer Love will come,
until He or She
is standing right in front of you –
your SoulMate.*

The In-Breath of God.
The Balancing of Love and Thought

I am here. I hold you tenderly, filling you with recognition of the Love of which you are made. I am here, alive in your creations as you are alive in Me, for Creation stretches forth from us outward in every direction without end.

I will speak to you about Creation, the most important subject that we have touched upon, for even your SoulMate will not "set your world a-right" if you do not understand Creation. As I draw you back to Me, on the winds of My In-Breath, something very important changes. You will be coming closer and closer to the truth of your being, because you will be coming ever closer to Me. So the proximity to the fires of Love that are the heart of My being, that which is your true and sacred Home, begin to change things.

In the book on SoulMate Love and Sacred Sexuality, I explained to you the nature of Love. I told you that Love is a fluid, molten substance. I also told you that we are working with the heat produced by Love, so that Love can move freely again in this world.

What you find in My heart is like the heat of a volcano. The Love that I am blazes forth to populate all of Creation, and to nourish absolutely All That Is, every moment for eternity. You can look at My Love as the energy of life, and then you will know how much Love I am—that all of Creation is continually fed with the energy of life from the heart of My being.

Your true home, beloved ones, is that molten, fiery Love, that great and passionate Love that illuminates all consciousness out of the substance of everything that I Am which is Love. So now, as you begin this journey of what we are calling "awakening," you will begin to see that *the changes taking place are mainly the changes that are occurring as you get closer in experience to the true, glorious, flowing heat of Love.*

I have explained to you that Love is the essence of My being, the substance from which all is made. Now, dear ones, we must speak about thought, for *thought is the consciousness that brings movement and shape to the Love. Without thought, there would be no action.* There would be no ideas to clothe with Love. There would be no energy to spark the Love that is My being and to bring forth Creation.

I have already told you how Creation began, when thought came forth and worked upon the ocean of Love that I am. It was My desire to share Love. It was My need to give Love that created the explosion that was the idea of Creation. The moment that thought touched the Love, a great reaction ensued, and every increment of thought that I had, every image that flashed through Me of billions of ways to give My Love became clothed in Love. In the great moment and by the energy that is thought, all of Creation came to be.

One great union of thought and Love, and Everything That Is came forth. Oh, it was indeed a "Big Bang," dear ones! It was smoke and fire and great whirling winds and billions of golden lights shooting forth in flight, taking on their form as the substance of Love wrapped around them. The further something flew from Me, the "cooler" the Love that clothed it became and, thus, the more dense or more physical. (This is an analogous explanation that is the best for your understanding at this time.)

Why have I explained all of this again? To explain to you this time, not the glory of Love, but *the power of thought.* Dear ones, in explaining this you will see just how amazing is that of which you are made. *You will see how critical it is that an understanding of thought be brought forth to humanity immediately and you will begin to grasp the power you have,*

My dearest beloved children. You will see how important it is to take hold of your heritage and to "make up your mind" to end the dream and to recognize who and what you are. Recognizing who you are, you can look upon your precious life and know that it is not a thing to waste. Know that it is a part of My very being, a part of My heart. Then you will, at last, begin the process of raising your reality back into what you might call that "Garden of Eden." You will realize how easily you can bring forth the change.

Let Me speak to you of thought, and let Me also make a request of each and every one of you. *For those who already understand these truths, the truth about thought, make it your mission to teach the importance of this topic to others in absolutely every way you can.* Do this without ceasing. Use every possible language.

My LightWorkers, this is the other half of the SoulMate information. *Love without control of thought is dangerous. If it is your dream that humanity be free, and if it is your dream that every human being have the gift of his or her SoulMate and the awakening it brings, then you must teach everyone about the power of thought and the need for control.* There must be a level of integrity, a level of responsibility to Creation before a human being can be allowed to have the powerful Love of their SoulMate. To give someone the most powerful access to the substance of

Love without a certain level of control is to place a generating station for anti-Love in the hands of those who would take advantage of this.

To those of you who are reading this, if you don't fully understand, I plead with you to stop right here and call to Me, and promise now, this moment, that you will pray and open and work with this until you understand the power of thought and your great responsibility.

Thought is energy that moves Love into creation. Thought is what takes Love and shapes it, moulds it, forms it into something. *Every thought creates.* Dear ones, there are two forces in Creation—Love and thought. From these, many energies and relationships have been formed. In My being, I who am Everything, it is the energy of thought upon the substance of Love that I am, that is who and what I am. All that has come forth from this interaction is all that now exists in movement, in form.

You, My beloved humanity, are My children. Thus, what is true for Me is true for you. *Love is that of which you are made (thus you are My heart). Thought is your creative energy with which you can move and mould and shape the Love – independently.* You are within My being, yes, but you, of all that is, can bring forth new life, even unto generating the very substance of Love. This is a very great gift. There is none else like you. It is also a very great responsibility. Everything else in this living universe is affected by the grand movements of thought upon Love. All but you choose their relationship to whatever is already happening as the current of life moves in and around them. They can act; they can react; they are in relationship. *But they do not create new Life. They do not generate new Love. Only you, My human children, can do this!*

And so you have! And you have done so mightily.

You have moved forth to gain independence that we might be close and might create together without you being drawn back into the ecstasy within Me. Your larger beings have poured forth their thoughts, and taking the Love that they generated, combined with their thoughts, they have been creative. Each of you is formed of Love. Each and every one of you can generate Love, and you can place your thoughts upon that Love (especially the love generated with your SoulMate) to create new life, new worlds, new civilizations.

Now is the time of My In-Breath. It is the time when the energy that is "farther away" from Me, this "slowed down or frozen" Love, is to be warmed back up. It is to be drawn back closer to My original center, the heart of which you are. Every part of human creation is included in this call.

The substance of all life is Love. All exists in Me. All is made of Me, and I Am Love. Consequently, dear ones, because the substance of Love is always there being acted upon (since Love is all there is), all human thought creates. All that is human is part of My heart, and thus are you always and ever a co-creative force.

What this means is that every thought that has ever gone forth (or in truth, is going forth in the Eternal Now, for Time is an illusion) is alive in Me. It has been created. It is a reality.

Yes, this can, at this level, be a scary thought. However, *as I now draw My In-Breath, bringing My children back into the full experience of My heart, everything created now must become aligned with Love.* If anything is not aligned with Love, it will be burned up by that molten Love that is within the center of My being.

This has been described in many ways, including in the Bible where it is said in ***Revelation*** that the Earth will be consumed by fire. ***This was simply the symbolic expression of what would happen to things not in alignment with Love as Creation drew back into ever-closer relationship with My true heart.*** For things not aligned with Love to be consumed by the intense heat of very "high frequency" Love is a natural part of the truth of life, of Creation. It is not a "big deal." It is just part of the law. You phrase this law as "what goes around comes around." ***As things are drawn back to Me, they meet the energy of their creation.*** It is a circle. Thus, ones whose creation has been filled with destruction and cruelty and hatred will be confronted by its vibrational reality as they "see themselves" in Me. Anything that is not Love does not last.

Until recently, this was the natural evolution for humanity as well. All of the spiritual information coming to the earth expressed this in one way or another. ***Now, dear ones, there is a new decision born of the LightWorkers' power of creation—that ALL creations will now be brought into alignment with Love! None are to be lost.*** This is a huge and amazing decision. And you, dear ones, have made this decision, whether you are conscious of doing so or not.

Thus, all creations will remain in form. ***All creations who can be aligned with Love in any way will be given continual existence and evolution***, the level of which will completely depend on the level of Love they can handle. ***Thus every creation ever brought forth will take its place in Creation at the distance from My center that it can survive.*** You, who are blossoming into divine Love, will be lifted up into the wholeness of your being and will come back into my deepest central heart, if you can remain in perfect alignment with Love.

Now, here is where I am going with this. Not only are you a creation of thought but ***every thought you have***

ever had is a developing creation as well. Creation continues inward unto forever, as well as outward into forever. Within you there are all levels of created beings brought forth by your thoughts, just as you too are a creation of thought. Whether you see these creations (your thoughts) as still within you or whether they have "gone forth," unless you have consciously uplifted and transformed them, they are in evolution now.

If you have a thought or cluster of thoughts that form a belief about yourself, those thoughts are a "personality" within you. As you move "upward" in your return to Me, what happens with them will affect you deeply. Ideally (and many of you have already done this, of course) you will consciously give them to Me to be uplifted back into pure Love. If you have done so, your upward journey will be easy.

But if you have not, as you are pulled closer to Me, when the heat (or you could call it "light" which is the manifestation of this heat) hits them, it will cause a bump in your road. If you are conscious, you will quickly understand what is happening, what part of you is being hit by the light, and you will consciously assist in its upliftment and transformation.

But if you are not aware, or for those not aware, it can manifest as illness, depression, or other discordant things happening in your life. If the person can open to Love and consciously allow the Love to come in, this conscious decision in itself will provide an expansion into Love for the inner personality or "thought bundle/belief."

Now, random thoughts that have gone out from a person have yet another story. They are still creations, but there have not been enough of them on a given topic to become a living "personality" or belief. These thoughts are like threads or ropes of energy going forth into the atmosphere. They do have an existence, but without enough energy to exist by themselves. They seek other like energies, where they can band together. These are what you think of as "thought forms." They are very real and very influential. As you already know, if a "pack" of negative thought forms is nearby and someone opens to that energy, not only does the thought "go forth" from its creator, but that thread that connects them can also be a conduit by which that whole "cloud" of thought can have access to the person who has opened to it.

Dear ones, every thought is a creation. Remember that thought is one of the two forces of creation. In other words, dear ones, thought is so powerful that with Love it is responsible for everything in Creation! I ask you to fully allow this to sink in. I also ask you now to understand fully and completely why controlling your thoughts is the highest priority. Not only is it the key to your fully conscious ascension into who you really are, but combined with Love it has the power to completely change your life. To change your world. To create anything and everything that you can imagine. Truly, anything you can think, you can create.

So as well as the reunion with the SoulMate, thought is the other half of the key. But while Love still resides purely in every person's heart, thought has been thwarted mightily. *It is truly unbelievable that in an entire world full of human beings, there is almost no awareness that thought creates reality!* Yes, some of you understand this, but let Me tell you, it is miniscule. Thus it is a pressing, pressing, pressing need. Until there is at least some ability to keep thought under control, it would actually be dangerous for some people to be united with their SoulMate. While the substance of everything is Love and thus all thoughts do create, the Love here on your planet is frozen enough that thoughts cannot destroy anything instantly (although when you look around your world, you see how well they can destroy!).

Consequently, any information about SoulMates is currently encoded with "safety" mechanisms. Yet, it being the goal to align every human being with Love, there is going to have to be instruction on "thoughts create reality" in a hurry. However, humanity is ready. This I can assure those of you whose hearts are confirming that you must help disseminate this critical piece. Many of the things happening on earth are expressly designed to assist people to get to the point where they know there has to be a change. Quickly. You will find that this information about thought will be welcomed hungrily as long as it is also filled with the warming energy of Love (which I can promise you is present here). This will help people feel hope and recognize Love as something in their reality (which is something many do not).

So, our messages will go forth with all of you who can take them, to give My beloved children the awareness of the Love that is now available for them in form, "in the flesh," as their SoulMate, as long as they will choose to gain control of their thought.

Dear ones, look around you. You will see millions of people in misery, overwhelm and lack, literally tossed up and down, up and down, by their thoughts. "Oh, it's a bad day," one will say. Or, "but he said something hurtful to me!" and this will begin a spiral of anger, hurt and isolation that completely colors their world and creates their reality—not to mention affecting the entire collective consciousness!

My beautiful children, the New World is here. It is calling you! All you need to do is claim your part, claim your existence as one of beauty, joy and Love. Begin building it, thought by thought, while lovingly lifting up all your earlier creations. Call for all of the assistance of those waiting to help you. The world of Love is so close now, closer than it has ever been, and now that you are in the In-Breath, coming Home, everything in Creation is being bathed continually in the light of My warming Love.

I am unfreezing your hearts, My beloved children. I am bringing Love as close to you as it can safely get. This I promise you. There are no exceptions. So all you have to do is choose to gain control of thought and to the degree that you accomplish this, to that degree exactly, will Love become your reality. Closer and closer Love will come, until He or She is standing right in front of you—your SoulMate.

But don't stop there! Keep going. Closer and closer still until you are flying upward together, back into your greater Reality, into the reunion of your true selves. Then you will begin to create. As you move ever more fully into the great, glowing Love that is My heart, you will be Home in the center of My being.

It is the truth, My beloved children, and it is accessible to you now. You! Each and every one of you, as soon as you choose. I challenge you to take your thoughts and make of every single one of them something great. Something you would be proud to bring to Me, your loving true parent. Something that you could say to Me, "Look, my beloved God, look what beautiful thing I have made!" And holding it out to Me, together we will fill it with Love. We will place it in the Womb of Creation that is the place where you are joined with your SoulMate, and we will bring it forth.

Then, thought-by-thought, you will learn how to create a world. How to create a universe. How to uplift your beloved Earth and your precious brothers and sisters. And, as we create with Love, you will see your beautiful fulfillment, your SoulMate, who is My Love for you made manifest. Ever more clearly will you be together. The All of Creation will be your playground in which you will joyously sow the seeds of Love and thought that are your destiny.

I want you serving
from the Heaven worlds,
showering Love
and living devotion and faith
so completely that it is only these moments
of great communion that matter.

The Next Shift: Becoming Love

I am here to lift your beautiful eyes, My
LightWorkers. You are walking on the cusp between the ego
and the heart. Yet even with all of your dedication, there is
more that I will ask of you. And even with all of your
understanding, there is more I would have you understand.
For as much as you desire to serve Me, it is not enough.
As much as you love your fellow human beings, it is
not enough.

Dear ones, it is only your ego that cares if we
successfully touch many lives. It is only your ego that is sad
when others do not understand or do not share your
spiritual path. It is only a heart still partially in the world
that could ever doubt or question the efficacy of its Love as
it is poured out upon the Earth.

***Dear ones, when you love enough, just the
opportunity to love will be your blessing.*** When you
worship Me in the fullness of your being, you will know
that these blessings are poured out upon the world. ***When
you are given to Me in every fiber of your being, it only
will matter that I am using you.*** You will know that
human minds do not need to hear or read My words for
human hearts to have received them.

When you have loved each other purely enough,
when your very cells sing out in glory, then you will trust
that real Love is all about giving completely and fully. You
will know that the Love that you share with your beloved
SoulMate will heal a thousand lives, will illuminate millions
of cells, will break the ice caps of hopelessness that float

upon the sea of human consciousness. It will be enough. No, more, far more than enough to have been allowed the blessing of such service as this.

You must "Love the Lord with all your heart and love your neighbor as yourself." In other words, it is the Christ in you that is the all of your desire, the fulfilling of your every need and wish, and the result of that passionate commitment is Love pouring forth on humanity.

Dear LightWorkers, there is a new level here awaiting you. Because *when you go forth for Me, beloved ones, you really must be as a hollow reed.*

When I send you into the world, you must be the crystal clear vessels of My light and My Love, the shining intelligence that is modeled after Me. You must be the perfect grace, bestowing only Love and never judgment of any sort. Not even the judgment that you deserve to be heard, or want to share your lives with those who will benefit from it.

Dear ones, I ask you each to open to this higher vision, the deeper awakening. *I want you serving from the Heaven worlds, showering Love and living devotion and faith so completely that it is only these moments of great communion that matter.* How can I explain this to you except to tell you that I will show you this Love.

When I explain that despite your dedication, most of you are not here yet, I do it only in the greatest tenderness and knowledge of your glory. Oh, there is certainly nothing derogatory! It is only that *you can be more.* You can live higher. *You can open more completely, until you are totally in line with My Will.* It is not that you will feel nothing or want nothing. It is that what you will feel and want will be only the movement of the most pure and perfect Love.

There is another shift here, My beloved ones. This is another point of giving up your smaller Will and turning every fiber of your being to the higher Will. When you do, you will be in the ecstasy of which I have spoken. You will be there absolutely continually. Passionately. Because it is only the ego that "brings you down." Down into any sense of limitation at all. Down into even a second's experience of things being anything other than perfect.

When you are truly giving, giving from your real heart center, you will have no expectations. When you have no expectations, then your entire being can be fully open to the higher mind, the movement of Love. But not only this, My beloveds, you will only be filled with the desire of the heart to live Love, to give Love so purely and passionately that this desire lights you up. In and of yourself you become a flaming torch lifted into communion with the realms of Love. Your entire being becomes "plugged in" to the flow of living Love.

Then, connecting with your SoulMate, the entire world is changed completely by your presence. Wherever you turn your attention, the entire vibrational make up of all around you changes. Where you walk, people will be lifted instantly. *They will see and experience the truth of Love from the upliftment of your presence. But you will not care if there is ever any recognition. Because just loving is total joy.* It is your glorious reality, where every increment of your being is continually lifted in songs of praise and worship.

In this state, dear ones, *there is no evaluator.* There is no consciousness within you that keeps a running commentary on people's responses, commentary on what you are hoping and how "reality" measures up. Commentary evaluating yourself. Commentary evaluating others. Commentary comparing the two. Commentary that sees any part of you! For if you "see" any part of yourself, you are in ego. The heart simply IS. Is joy. Is ecstasy.

From this place where you currently reside vibrationally, it is only a little leap for some of you to this new residence. Yet it can be that leap that can seem impossible to span. The kind where you get "closer" and "closer" but the distance ever divided by half is never covered. Thus, My beautiful ones, *life events that do not meet your expectations are a call to you to leap into My arms.* Eliminate the distance. Become the Shift. You can keep "getting closer" forever. I call you now to simply BE HERE.

Can you sense this new experience where Love lives you? I ask you to push yourselves over the edge and into My arms. For you cannot live in the old mind anymore. Though many of you have chosen to live above the ego, I now come to push you further! I come to push you beyond ego completely.

I do not tell you what you will have or not have. Because as long as you function from a mindset that contains this dichotomy, your ego is present with you. Rather, I ask you to make a leap into a world of Love in which *Love is all that is.* Love. Pouring through you so perfectly that *every definition of yourself dissolves.* Will you be able to "function" like this? Absolutely. And once you do, you will understand many of the symbolic stories contained in the various earthly Holy Books. The "parting of the Red Sea" is simply this change, for everywhere you step, the vibration of everything around you turns to Love.

Thus you will walk right through any negativity and for the time you are there, it will cease to exist. And not only this, My beloved ones, every person your energy touches will experience his own perfection for as long as you are in the vicinity. Thus what you could spend lifetimes trying to put into words will be given to people as an experience. You will know how your Love is used, just as Jesus knew of the woman whose bleeding stopped when she touched the hem of his garment.

My dearest LightWorkers, you cannot settle for less than everything. You cannot settle for a "normal" life, one in which you look at the world as two beings: the observer and the observed. This is what I mean by the inner evaluator. I ask you now to switch your identity–each one of you. *Come back to the full awareness that you are My heart. That together, each with your SoulMate, you are loving as I love. You are My heart, pouring forth Love absolutely without any qualifications, ever.* For you know, don't you, how I love? I do not even see anything but Love.

When I look upon each one of you, dear ones, every single human being, I see only a cell in My heart. And what is My heart but Love? Beating in Love, being Love, holding forth Love as the one truth. This is why you have read that I love even those who have lived in terrible darkness. Why? The darkness is invisible to Me. When I look upon any human being, Oh, I am so in Love with each and every one of you! Just as a human mother gazes upon her perfect newborn child and falls in Love, so it is, magnified, exponentially, when I gaze into you. Beloved ones, the only thing that darkness does is keep you, My humanity, from seeing who you are.

Now I ask you to see My children as I do. No comparisons. No evaluations. And no judgments of yourselves. *Dear ones, nothing has to be "done" or learned anymore. Everything now is about choosing your identity as Love.* Do this and you will be in Love with your bodies and with your selves. Passionately, tenderly, in absolute joy and gratitude for the body's generous support of you, allowing your presence here, in physicality. *This relationship of Love will draw perfection. Period.* You do not need to "hold images in your mind" of what you want that perfection to be. How limiting! *How "on Earth" (or in Heaven) could your smaller mind possibly know what your real perfection is?* So even this must shift—even the way you believe you create.

Become only Love. Share only Love together. Then Love will be your reality. Love will be completely who you are. What you are. Where you are. Then you just experience every perfect moment.

If you *are* Love in action, then you can know that each thing you do, every word you say, every action you take will be done in perfect Love. Thus there will be no need to evaluate. Then, dear ones, as Love moves forth in you, so too will this Love, My Love, your Love – there is no difference – begin to call all of our humanity. The words will literally move through you. The "trumpet call" will issue forth from your being and thus will a perfect cascade of words and light and images pour forth from you, forming itself to reach humankind. You will now be perfect Love in action.

I cannot send you forth, My LightWorkers, with judgment left in you. Judgment of yourselves or judgment of others. But don't worry – send you forth I will. Oh, I ask a lot of you, but you have always known I would. So with every seeming "adversity," remember that it is a call to LOVE MORE — to "flip over" to the reality of Love; to see and know the glorious truth within yourselves, within each other and within every human being.

I charge you with the responsibility of perfect Love

(remember what "response – ability" says). These words I have spoken to you may be worse than gibberish to the majority of humanity at this time. Yet they hold a vibration for you of a very important shift to make. When you make it, *you will be Love's voice.* And Love will speak through you.

Dear ones,
I promise you
that almost no human being on Earth
has ever been looked at
with true Christ-like unconditional Love.
This is what I am growing
in My Light Workers —
that you look upon every one of
My beautiful children
and see them with Christ eyes,
with Christ heart.

What is Given in Secret Will Be Rewarded Openly.
Moving into Christ Consciousness

I am here, My beloved ones. I come again to speak to you and through you, to all whose lives touch yours intimately. I can promise you that there are no accidental associations. Those who are open to this Love that I pour through you are literally accepting the key to the lock on the door to eternal Love. And of course they are first accepting through their recognition, the key to the knowledge of their own hearts.

Beloved LightWorkers, know this. Know that you are a gift that I am offering to My children. Know, too, that they may accept this gift or they may turn away and in either case, you must bless them. Know also that *it can only matter to you that you have the opportunity to bless! It cannot matter to you if they accept or reject, understand or turn away.*

It is this that I will now talk about, for this is a subject of the greatest importance. It is the cusp of this awakening upon which you are now standing, and it is for this shift that all are breathlessly waiting. Dear ones, you are experiencing the held breath of God. Not My Out-Breath, yet not quite My In-Breath. I come to accomplish the shift in your inner landscape that will bring each of you into the deepest communion with Me. The glorious and joy-filled inner landscape that is your inheritance. The landscape through which there flows the crystalline waters of living truth and the joyous reunion with Me.

Dear ones, this held breath is to teach you so that you will each move closer and closer and closer to Me. In this stillness of the held breath, I come to tell you the truth. *It is only in giving forth My Love that you will receive, and that all that you receive comes only from Me.*

Now you may stop here and say to Me, "Oh, but I know this." And if you do, I must gently say that you do not. You do not know it so completely that you are not present in the equation. *Beloved ones, most of you do not yet fully trust Me to do all good and to provide all good. Even more importantly, you have not drawn so close to Me that I am everything to you.* Not yet. But you are listening. You are saying "yes!" You are reaching forth your hand to Me and saying "yes"—to being free of ego in every moment.

Dear ones, you must know that your sustenance, your good comes directly from Me. Not from yourselves. Most of the books on "manifesting" will tell you that you can manifest what you need and want, and that you can precipitate from Divine Substance all that you need. Dear ones, I want to correct this.

It is true that you are co-creators and by the power of your Will and vision you can create. But (please listen) this is not all I want for you! For beloved ones, you do not have a high enough vision. You cannot even imagine how much I can give to you. How much I want to give to you; how much I long to give to you. *If you envision your highest good, dear ones, it will not be good enough!* And it will require effort to sustain it, to bring it forth. And, as well as needing to keep applying your visualization and your awareness, dear ones, it will not bring you close enough to Me.

When you know that ALL you have I give to you, then you must draw close to Me. You must draw close so that you are available for Me to give to. You must draw close so you can come to know how much I love you and thus how much I long to give and give and give to you. You then will also understand that all you must do is open to receive.

This is true—how I love you and how I will give to you abundantly. There are, however, two criteria. The first one is your accepting what I give, as I have been saying, and secondly, *r*ealizing completely that I am your only source. This is the most important change in thinking that you must now accomplish. Nothing will necessarily change in the "outer" in any obvious way, not at first. Your "livelihood" will still seemingly come from the same sources as it does now on the physical plane. But you must not ever believe this. I ask you to completely disassociate the two—for only then will you be open to the next larger steps as I teach you how to accept My abundance in ever-larger ways.

IT IS IN GIVING THAT YOU RECEIVE. What I want you to understand is that there is a higher plane upon which this law is now functioning. Not in the easy and obvious physical plane giving. Dear LightWorkers, anyone can do this and many do who are completely wrapped up in ego. No, this law also now moves inside of you. It now becomes a higher law which is that *you become My Will to give.*

Dear ones, here is the difference that I am showing you now. I am no longer asking you to "control your thoughts," to "create your reality," to visualize or even to "work toward" being free of ego. No, beloved ones. *You have reached the most powerful possibility: the shifting of your Will into Mine.* I ask you to become so close to Me that you know that My Will is your magnificent good. I ask you to know that My Will—through you—is the upliftment of humankind and the blessing and abundance of My children in ways you could never dream. So the difference becomes a union of Love that is so powerful and poignant that even the concept of ego disappears.

How do you accomplish this shift? *You give without ceasing at the highest level you can reach.* Give at the highest level that is consuming to you, that will blanket your inner landscape completely and come pouring forth continually from you. Soon, very soon, you will become aware that I am giving through you, that I am "upgrading" your giving and empowering it mightily. You will begin to sense the power flowing forth from you. But *I will gift you with this awareness only when it does not matter to you.* At first your giving forth does need to be done only for the sake of doing it. However, though you may not understand what your giving is accomplishing, you will immediately experience My presence.

This giving I am speaking of, dear LightWorkers, is the unseen variety. It does need to be silent giving of the inner light and energy. Each can choose what works best for you. It can be *prayer without ceasing.* I recommend this at first because it will draw all of your attention to all the amazing possibilities for giving blessing and prayers of assistance. It can be *sending Love directly from the heart.* This will currently take at least some sort of visualization practice in order to fully sustain it. It can be *sending of healing energies* but it must be from you with the goal of accomplishing such a flow of energy that I am invited to lift you and carry your intention into My higher Will. "Priming the pump" is an apt explanation. In other words, *this giving must originate from your Will with your Will being to do My Will.* I am asking you to give so much, to give so perfectly, to give such Love with such purity that you are joined with Me. Thus it should not be asking other beings to work through you.

This giving, this praying without ceasing, is a way of life. It is your inner landscape. It is a continual scan for anything and anyone that you can bless. In doing this, you do take hold of My Love. You do take hold of the Christ light, and the ego disappears within it. And as you give, so will you receive, so as you pour forth blessings every single moment, so will there be blessings poured into you.

Dear ones, as you make this shift in your awareness, as you leave the realm of ego and enter the realm of Christ, then you will be ready. Then you will be ready to do My Will on Earth, and to completely be the blessing of humanity every single moment. Then you will be ready for Me to use you to light the world. *I can promise you that you have not yet known joy until you are truly giving.*

This giving does not need to be physical. In fact it generally should not be physical. It must be "not seen by the eyes of men" until it is tested and tried in the chamber of your heart. And of course, as you "lay hold" of the light of Christ, all else held in that light will be revealed to you.

Dearest ones, I ask that your shift be a personal relationship with Me. Not just a relationship with some principles of spiritual awakening, but with Me. I have a personal relationship with Christ. Didn't Jesus continually speak of this? Well, if all of you are to be the embodiment of Christ for this age, if this awakening is the recognition of your life in Me, then does it not become obvious that we are to have a personal relationship?

Now, this shift into Christ Consciousness, the inner giving that will become your way of life, is not something yet available to the majority of human beings. Most will be opening to Love embodied in their SoulMate. But the Christ Consciousness is available to you, My LightWorkers. And by reason of greatest necessity, I ask you to claim it quickly. It is imperative that I show forth its glorious possibilities, even if the majority cannot yet understand it.

Dear ones, with a few exceptions of course, almost every spiritual teacher that comes into the limelight becomes somehow tainted by the experience. So humanity, in general, has come to expect it. (Listen carefully.) Thus, as each of you as LightWorkers goes forth to teach, you will be dealing with the very powerful energy of the mass consensus that spiritual teachers "fall." You might believe yourselves impervious. I can assure you that in your present state you would not be impervious. Thus, I come now to lift you beyond this. So you may consider this an "intensive."

After a month or so of practice, I would like you to begin to test the waters of your inner reality. With "ruthless" honesty, assess whether your entire being holds only blessings in every situation. In any situation that created a loss in elevation, you will grasp this message, the living thereof, ever more deeply.

This realm of Christ Consciousness is the complete transfer of your entire inner reality into the living embodiment of My Love as I pour you forth upon the world. All of the things that you know, you now must begin to live. Remember what I am showing you and it will be easy.

♥ I pour My gifts upon you. I love you so much, so deeply and so personally that I am giving everything to you, every moment.

♥ The way to receive these gifts is to "prime the pump" with continual giving. Bless without ceasing, pulling both My gifts and My Will for My Love into your life.

♥ This process, done with the awareness of who you are, is your shift into Christ Consciousness.

♥ What is given "in secret" will be rewarded openly. The giving that is necessary here is giving that only you and I know that you are doing.

♥ You will accomplish the conscious connection with Christ, the acceptance of your heritage as My Love, My heart in motion in the world.

♥ Giving is the key to receiving on every level. Giving Love reveals your SoulMate. It also reveals your identity as Christed beings.

♥ If you will to do My Will, you will quickly come Home because My Will is the perfection of our Love. In every way, My Will is a bigger, greater good than you can currently see.

♥ Giving is not only the key to receiving. It is also the key to bliss, to ecstasy, to joy, to having every part of your being in true happiness.

♥ Everything is in intimate relationship. So while your destiny is far bigger than the "personal" experience of your ego, in a different sense everything is completely personal. You have a completely personal relationship with Me. I am right here, loving you. And the more you give forth blessings, the more you pray without ceasing (silently), the more you will experience My presence. And the more you will understand our relationship. Are you ready?

What is Christ-level humility?
It is the absolute conviction that
all of My children are equal in My eyes.
You are to love as Christ loves –
meaning that you simply
ARE My Love.
You accomplish this
by giving Me your heart,
completely and fully,
keeping nothing for yourself.

Praying Gratitude

*D*ear ones, I pour My Love upon you. It is a joy to see your prayers intensify, your hearts beginning to bear the true light. It is a wonder to behold your pure longing— longing to love deeply, to open your hearts that I may love through you.

Thank you, My LightWorkers, for your prayers. Thank you for realizing what I am saying, for growing your hearts to encompass it. Thank you, each one, for the increase in your determination and the dedication of your Love.

Some of you have prayed to know how to become the hollow reed, how to have only the experience of My Love living in you, loving as you. You have prayed how to have only My Love seeing every person within your range of vision. I have heard your prayer. But, beloved ones, I hear the prayers of your heart long before they reach your mind, so I am ever leading you to discover the prayers that you need to pray.

What I want this message to say to you is that I know what you need. I know what you need long before you need it. Thus I even know what prayers your heart and mind must speak, what recognitions you must gain until your purpose is fulfilled.

Knowing this, I ask that you place your Will into Mine, again and again. Every hour of every day. For though you could teach yourself everything you need to know, it would take you so much longer. And though you can learn to direct the various elements, the flows and tides of life, you cannot at this level know the majesty of My Will for you. My good for you. Even the prayers that are timely each step of the way.

So your first step, every morning of every day and every moment that follows, is that I ask that you make sure that the pinnacle of your relationship together is Me, is My Will. Beloved ones, without placing your Will into Mine and releasing it, you will not know what it even means to embody the glorious energies that you are. I can promise that as you fully begin to live in My Will as Divine Masculine and Divine Feminine, you will take on the full mantle of Christ. You will be My Love made manifest.

As you fully embody the truth of these energies, dear ones, you will finally recognize yourselves. This may seem to be an odd statement, but it is true. Remember how I told you that many marriages fail because one or both people remember. They remember the SoulMate and feel that the human partner doesn't measure up.

As you begin to both take on/embody this divine nature of your charge, something amazing will happen in your relationship and in your inner world. Dear ones, you will recognize your partner and you will recognize yourself. As the Divine Masculine and Divine Feminine become expressed in you, at last the memory and the reality fit together.

All of your life you have waited for the touch of true and tender Love and the ensuing ecstasy. Now, at last, it is beginning to happen to many of you. With it comes a deep joy. A deep satisfaction. A feeling that at last all is right with your world. How does it feel? As though you are Home in each other's arms. ***This, dear ones, is how it is going to be*** *for every single human being as each accepts the Love he or she is, and draws forth the SoulMate.*

Many wonderful things will come from this, of course. One of the greatest, dear ones, will be a world filled with contentment. What happens when you have contented, joy-filled, loved human beings? There is no need for war. There is no drive to negate your brother, to put down your sister, for there can be no jealousy. There will be no envy. Dear ones, the entire profile of humanity will dramatically change as people experience even a little of their SoulMate relationship. Is this not a revelation? A great blessing? Is this not the doorway opening into the New World? The answer is a resounding YES. It is.

Another glorious thing that will happen as you embody the Divine Masculine and Divine Feminine is that you will recognize yourself. Now if you don't think this is important, let Me tell you that it is. Beloved ones (pay attention - it's exciting!), almost no one on Earth who is human truly loves self. I can assure you this is the truth. Oh yes, people work toward it continually. Counselors and psychiatrists, shamans and healers, priests and everyone in between are continually flooded by a stream of people who cannot find themselves in their own heart.

These beloved ones try many things. They do psychodrama. They say affirmations. They continually look at their poor parents, all of their lovers, their colleagues—you name it—trying to find a way to love themselves. Yet underneath, it does not change. Can you guess, dear ones? Of course. ***They cannot love themselves because they know what they really are meant to be.*** Dear ones, every atom of your being remembers, even if your mind does not. So here are My sweet children. They look at themselves and they see this overriding ego. They see jealousy and anger. They see scheming and comparisons. They see vengeance, be it big or little. They see anxiety, depression, desperation. All of it. And they do not recognize this being. Who is this person who is such a "mess"? Their heart cries out to them. So even if it isn't conscious, the remembrance is there, and nothing measures up. I know, dear ones. I placed the memory in you in the very cells of light that are your being. I had to. While it brings you suffering and conflict, dearest beloveds, you had to remember who you are.

So here is the great, good news. The moment you say, "Yes," to Love and your heart begins to open, you begin to recognize yourself. There is a soft sigh of relief. "Oh, thank God," your heart breathes. "I am not only that cut-off, manipulative person." "Oh, thank you, God," you cry, looking heavenward.

Now that this has happened for those of you awakening, you now come to the next step. This is where you are today. You feel your world coming right. You find glimpses of your real self. You begin to have moments of ecstasy and moments of true self-acceptance because you now see the real you peeking through. But now, suddenly, having the comparison, you really begin to see the ego. It is fully "in your face." Thus you begin your fervent prayers. And thus *I lead you, giving you the descriptions of the hollow reed,* for, dear ones, I too am ready. I am ready to pour through you to the world. To nurture and nourish. I am ready for every couple to take hold of Christ. To become the true light of Love. To live free of the ego.

So once again you question Me, "God, how do we get there from here?" This time, dear ones, there is an answer for you. Rather than a leap, there is a pathway. And as you walk this pathway together with your SoulMates, you will see yourselves ever more clearly. You will then find a miracle within you—a glorious circle of self-Love, a gift of full acceptance with completely open heart, first of each other, then of yourself. As your SoulMate Love blossoms, as your SoulMate touches you, your very atoms will awaken in Love. Your heart will sing exuberance as it sees the other half of itself. So Love will pour forth from you through the open floodgates. Your SoulMate will be recognized. And you will be giving. Giving of Love in your highest, fullest capacity, which, of course, brings that very Love back to you. You are washed in Love. Your very being is bathed in the warming joy of your beloved's touch. Love becomes your experience. Hourly. Daily. As you fall in Love with your SoulMate ever more fully, so dear ones will you begin to truly love yourself. You will take a stand against the ego, and then powered by the SoulMate Love, you will rise above the ego, transforming it in the blessings of your Love.

This is one thing that happens as you claim your identity and embody the Divine Masculine and Divine Feminine. But there is one more piece, dear ones, of great importance. You must transform your mind into the mind of Christ, for thought creates reality. So even though you love in purity and even though you love in honor of your beloved SoulMate, there is another facet. There is something that you must choose to change, to gain "enlightenment." Yes, you have all heard this word used thus before, but dear ones, in this case it is very appropriate, for *your thoughts and your Love are the two ingredients of change, riding upon the energy of your Will.*

Dear ones, the ego came to life to strengthen you as individuals. It came into being to forge a separate identity. It was designed, as you know, to keep you from melting back into Me. Thus, it has surprising strength. This strength was a necessity, of course. In most cases it is not going to simply go away, even in the face of Love. As you know it has become strengthened beyond our expectancy.

When you pray to Me to be only a channel for My

Love, I now whisper to you that this will be a little journey. I have spoken to you of judgment, which is the ego's main tool. And of course, the ego operates on the vibrational level below the heart.

Dear ones, I recently asked you to pray without ceasing. This, dear ones, is the journey. *It is the choice to fill the mind in such a way that it engages the heart,* and this engagement will lift you over judgment and into the mind of Christ, which is, dear ones, a mind bathed in living Love. It is a mind that becomes ever joined with the heart so that judgment and ego cannot exist in it any more. It is a mind in which the heart will not allow the vibration to fall below its frequency of Love.

In order to accomplish this, dear ones, I ask you to accomplish a melding of such devotion and focus that it is by your desire, your focus, your Will and dedication that *mind and heart become fused in My Will forever more.*

Thus you must fill your mind with the heart's great urgency of Love. This is the passion that lives within you. *I now call you to a passion of prayer of such strength and intensity that it can accomplish your ego's transformation.* To do this, dear ones, you are now ready for the upgrade of your prayer. *Dear ones, it is now time to pray without ceasing in gratitude.* Now I will explain what I mean.

Your prayers, dear ones, are beautiful. As you have swept the world, both personal and impersonal, you have prayed the most beautiful prayers. I have been greatly moved, and the angels have been sent into gales of rejoicing song. This is the truth. With every utterance of sincere prayer, with every silent prayer, which is even greater potency, oh, dear ones, everything around you is changed. You do not yet see what an impact this has had, even in the short time since I introduced it as your call to becoming the

Christ in Me.

You have changed so much you are ready to change again. Yes, please, bow your heads in gratitude, for that is coming next. Beloved ones, here is the truth of prayers of gratitude and in it the greatest keys for change. ***Gratitude must never be limited to what already is.***

Most people when praying gratitude (this is how we will refer to it—"praying gratitude," for as with Love, gratitude is a universal force)—most who think of gratitude (which of course is far too few), begin to give thanks for what they have, what is in them and in their lives. Now certainly, this is a good thing, for gratitude truly does unite the mind and the heart within you. And of course, this is a source for change.

However, dear ones, if you will remember, I have explained to you that the greatest law is Giving. Giving, giving, giving. If there is one word that creates heaven, this is the word. GIVING. Yet prayers of gratitude are usually about the self.

Here is the sweet and tender shift, dear ones, introduced before, but now I bring it forth to you like a princess in great array of glittering beauty. It is like the force of Love that will be Queen as you take it within you and make it the ruler of your inner kingdom. ***Here is the pathway to the living mind of Christ. It is to pray without ceasing in gratitude for others.***

Oh, dear ones, catch hold of this. Catch hold and ride it upward to the stars of your being. Let it launch you into the incarnation of your Love. And may you realize that such gratitude—gratitude in every area of your life—is a communion of the SoulMates, for the gratitude itself, which I called the Queen of our inner kingdom, is the embodiment of the Divine Feminine. And dear ones, the power of Will that sends it forth and thus brings it to life, is the Divine Masculine. So just as in physical procreation, it is the seed of the man that brings movement/life into the circle, the ovum, of the female.

So, dear ones, as you pray gratitude together, in the many ways that I will show you, you are creating the Holy Family. Together as a couple you are giving birth to Christ.

Praying gratitude will become the sum of your beings, dear ones. It supercedes everything you have used to bring you here—affirmations, breath-work, all other forms of thought control, which of course were imperative to your growth. All of this was needed to bring you to the point that the Christ mind may now take root in you—or perhaps more accurately, that together you are now "pregnant with the light of Christ."

Praying gratitude for yourselves and your SoulMate is beautiful and important. But I now want to focus on praying for others, because what you give comes back to you. So as you pray gratitude for others, you are covering your own. Not that you want to skip any prayers of gratitude, ever.

Dear LightWorkers, there are two elements of praying gratitude for others. They both fall under the over-arching element of "pray without ceasing." The first is gratitude for the person, or people. This is the movement into the experience of My mind. If you think about this, you will realize that this is how I think, and as you become it, you become the mind of Christ. You know that Christ is the embodiment, the manifestation in the world of My Love. So when you begin to pray gratitude for someone, simply think to yourself, "How would God see this one, or these two, or this group?" Open to your heart and allow the experience to become you. I will lift you. I will show you this person in My eyes. I will show you how much I love that person.

I will show you how tenderly I love them and how any tiny opening, any little peek of hope or spiritual awareness, is so precious that I rush forth in response to support and magnify it. You will find tears of joy pouring forth from your eyes at the goodness of such recognition, and at the deep gladness I have at their presence in the world and every little opening to the light.

The more you do this, the more you will see people as they are in Love. And so you finally cease creating negativity through all the judgments you have always had as a way of relating to people. Of course, you know that whatever you hold in your mind, especially if your heart is in any way engaged, you create. Thus, most people continually create negativity about their fellow man every single time they even look at another person. Is it any wonder the world is so confused? The ego is still so strong? And, dear ones, is it any wonder people have such a struggle in growing into Love when you are all constantly bombarding each other with negative thoughts?

Dear ones, you are creating the negativity in your brother or sister's life as you pass judgment, even subtly! And because whatever is sent forth does come back to the sender (this I absolutely promise you is true), then you are creating such a difficult road for yourself at the same time. Thoughts may wound, inhibit, influence and interfere. Dear ones, negativity is rampant on Earth. As the vibrations are lifted higher, thoughts travel more easily, more swiftly. Is it any wonder then, as the population becomes denser and superficiality becomes the norm (negativity without the amelioration of spiritual sustenance), that more and more people are taking tranquilizers and anti-depressants? They are trying to compensate for the thought bombardment.

The second element of praying gratitude for others is very important. It is gratitude for their gifts. This means two things. It means the obvious—praying gratitude for all the good that others receive. This should be obvious to you —what better way to come up over the ego than to be in continual gratitude for every tiny thing that is good in their lives. The ego thrives on jealousy. People are usually filled with the ego's secret wish—for the failure of others, for their lack of success because it makes the ego feel superior. Some of you may have seemingly moved past this. To this I say that it is often only pushed into the subconscious. Whatever your experience, I who know all can assure you that the majority of humanity is still very much in this. So to pray fervently in gratitude for the good of others truly pulls the rug right out from under the ego!

The second part of gratitude for others' gifts is to be completely grateful for what they will become—for what they will have, as the good you know I want for them comes into their lives. This will be familiar to you. It is a form of co-creation. This is how you "have faith in things not seen." This is how you manifest good. Now you certainly should use this for yourselves as well. Thank Me for that which you have prayed to receive, thus anchoring its arrival here on Earth. You may still pray the request for the gift that you want for yourselves and others, but it should be only a small percentage of your prayers. Better, of course, is to request the manifestation of My Will for you. Once again, you cannot even begin to picture the magnitude of the good I want for you. Prayers of request have too much room for ego.

Thus to pray gratitude is definitely to put yourself in right relationship with life. It is looking at the highest vision, and lifting yourselves into the pure, proven energy of gratefulness.

As you pray these prayers of gratitude, I will be with

you. For such is the vibration of gratitude that it is the most refined of current human relationship. The more you pray gratitude, the closer we will be, the more you will be filled with Me, filled with My Love, seeing with My mind, and becoming My deep loving and passionate tenderness as I lift you, My children. As you glimpse again and again just how much I love every one of you, you will be forever changed, for as you see it again and again, you will begin to accept My Love. Then you will be attuned with My heart—and Christ will come to dwell in you.

I will teach each of you. Tenderly and carefully. I will place the seed within you for the birthing of the Christ.

Dear ones,
when you love enough,
just the opportunity to love
will be your blessing.
When you worship Me
in the fullness of your being,
you will know that these blessings
are poured out upon the world.
When you are given to Me
in every fiber of your being,
it only will matter that I am using you.
You will know that human minds
do not need to hear or read My words
for human hearts to
have received them.

Co-Creation Through Praying Gratitude: The Next Step

I am here, of course. I am here as joy begins to show itself to you as everything in your world. Truly, as your hearts are Love, and as you experience the deep inner joy of living in harmony with the river of spirit as it pours through you, so will your world reflect it. As you are experiencing (and you are just beginning!), when your inner world is filled with the experience of gratitude, your outer world becomes more and more and more filled with all that makes you grateful. It becomes filled, dear ones, with good and more good, for which your hearts will sing their praise to Me. Such praise of course will lift your world, refining the very vibration of your being and then everywhere you look, you will see more good. This, dear ones, is en-light-en-ment. Everything within becomes light. Everything without comes to reflect that light, which in turn brings more inner light. So it grows.

As your Love increases, as you choose gratitude, you do attune yourselves to that glorious flow of giving that is the hallmark of true spirituality. So you will find yourselves sharing this experience of true spiritual family—sharing the experience, dear ones, of true and actual grace. And what is grace? It is when you accept My gifts for you, and thus accepted, the light within you and the light without are balanced, and you become the full expression of God as you.

Yet, beloved ones, in saying this, you must understand the depth of this experience to which you are called. What does this mean to live in grace? And most importantly what does it mean when I ask you to do My Will?

I am beginning to open this to you. I will take your hands and touch your hearts, and I will build with you a vision of who you are becoming. I will talk to you about co-creation, about what it means to be My children. Most importantly, I will open the secret chambers in both your heart and your mind and teach you what it means to meld the two. Not only what it means to gain the mind of Christ by lifting thought into union with Love. I will show you the last step: becoming true co-creators with Me. Truly, you are My children. As it is with human children of mortal parents, it is the great hope in the heart of a parent that the child will live the parents' greatest possibilities. Dear ones, My beloved heart, I now whisper to you that this is true with Me also.

In you there can be All That I Am multiplied. Can you sense this? Can you feel how this knowledge lives ever in Me—that every one of you can wave your hand across the skies and leave trails of stars and moons and planets? That you too can bring forth progeny that can hold the perfection of universes in their consciousness? Just think for one moment. If every single human being said, "Yes!" to all they are, think of how much Love could be brought into existence every moment! Oh, you cannot yet imagine it for you cannot even touch the possibilities within yourselves. But let Me assure you, it would be great. How I cherish this thought, for I *can* see. I can see Love bursting forth exponentially, second by second—multiplying, pouring forth in great cascades. Every single mind it touches is awakened, just like Sleeping Beauty. You may smile, yet you can see the course of a potential future I am waiting upon you to bring forth.

Step by step, dear ones, we are building your new inner life. I am giving you the avenues for aligning yourselves to the truth of who you are—the Love that is My heart. I have spoken to you of taking hold of your heritage. Of gently, but with determination, choosing to become the embodiment of Love, the manifested heart and mind of Christ. And, oh, as you have taken this in, as your hearts have said "yes," we have moved closer. Closer. Closer. Until you can become the hollow reed and I can pour through you perfectly.

Now I bring you one more step. Where we stopped in our last exploration of claiming the Christ mind, of living as Christ, the living manifestation of My Love, was praying gratitude. Now we will explore gratitude, doing My will, and your role as co-creators. You may ask the question: if you are turning your Will over to Me and asking to do My Will for you, as you, then what of all of My earlier statements that you are to be co-creators? Did I not create you in order to share creation? In order to have an equal consciousness that can reflect back to Me who I am in an expanded way?

I will answer this question on the highest level you can currently absorb. But please listen when I tell you that you must keep asking this question because you are a work in progress, a flower just beginning to blossom. There is no way to really show you yet all of what you can be. As you claim whatever you can understand and take it into your life to live it, only then will it begin to grow before you. Only then will the next step be revealed. Dear ones, please remember this. Everything you learn as I lead you ever closer to Me must be brought forward into your life in order for you to know it. Let Me repeat Myself to you. *Everything, beloved ones, everything that is the treasure of your being, the truth of your miraculous heritage in Me, each and every one must be embodied in you in order for you to claim it.*

This you may already understand, but you do not yet

grasp the personal nature of it. You know that all great energies must be embodied. My Love , the Christ—exemplified so beautifully by Jesus—now must be embodied in humanity, as must the energies of planets, energies of the elements, and of Nature. Now you must draw this more carefully into your consciousness. ***The only way to claim any of the things I show you—the qualities, the Love, and most of all the GIVING—is to bring it into the world in you as action in your life.*** In other words, beloved ones, you cannot raise something up until you have grounded it as you on this (ever less) physical plane. Even great energies cannot serve if they are not embodied.

Dear ones, part of your understanding of the miracle of the coming of Christ AS humanity is going to be your ability to see and know, to honor and work in respect and harmony with all the beautiful beings who are embodying energies for the world. For the Earth. For humanity. This is going to be part of coming awake; realizing just how deeply you share this Creation with glorious sentient beings who are the embodiment of the very energies you need to understand. Thus, instead of valiantly lifting the burden and being independent, which is the current limiting ego-consciousness, you will come into deeply honoring all those with whom you share life.

It is so important for humanity to make this shift out of the egocentric human consciousness (which sees itself as the only possible intelligent beings) to the unity consciousness of the truth. The truth, beloved ones, is again far too limited by words, but your heart will experience it. It is the fact that you are living in an extraordinary weaving of consciousness, supporting and enlightening and growing each other.

What does it mean to live in My Will? For what I have asked of you is that you release your Will into Mine.

Then I have asked you to pray without ceasing and more specifically to pray gratitude. My answer to you is this.

My Will for you is for you to be co-creators with Me. My Will for you is that you will recognize the truth of who you are. You are the embodiment of My Love already. You are My heart. ***Dear ones, you already are the embodiment of My Love.*** I am saying this to you so you will understand it, thus I repeat it. Please sit for a moment and take this in. ***There is nothing you have to create from scratch.*** There really is nothing you must struggle to build. In truth you do not have to work your way up through all sorts of life lessons to gain even an inkling of what you are. That is only a belief.

My beloved children, you already are it. You are Christ. You are My Love. Everything else has been a moment of forgetting, but of course forgetting with a purpose. A moment of forgetting to develop your strong individual identity so you can remain aware of yourselves as individuals without melting back into Me in bliss. The other reason, dear ones, is so you will appreciate, oh, truly appreciate everything as you awaken. If you do, if you pour Love into every single being upon whom your gentle awareness touches, you will create the New World right there.

What I want to explain to you is that I truly am giving you the keys to Christ Consciousness. For coming Home, beloved ones, is truly as simple as remembering who you are. In remembering to bless every being you find before your consciousness, you simply function as a cell of My heart. This function is to allow My Love to pour through you. This, dear ones, is actually accomplished by praying gratitude in the form of gratitude for every being's perfection.

Can you see, dear ones, that as you are My Love, conscious and manifested, then you have the ability to bring into the world, to manifest My Love through this embodiment? Right? This is the function of My heart, to love. So as you accept or claim the truth of your being, My Love pours through directly and you guide it through your consciousness—your prayers of gratitude.

Yet you are individuals also, the joy of My creation. So as well as simply allowing Me to use you, which would be doing My Will, you are also to co-create. Many believe that being co-creators is to decide what you want and then ask Me to help you. It is more than this. Often those who see this way unknowingly are creating with the ego. Until every one of you, beloved ones, has completely overcome the ego, it will find truly a million ways to sabotage your very best intentions. You will start by believing you are creating in Love and before you know it you are creating separation, or creating for self instead of for others. Oh, most insidious. You may believe you are motivated by giving when in truth underneath you are motivated by getting.

If you are in any way motivated incorrectly, dear ones, it will damage both of us, for you will step forth and embody energies that are the reverse of Love, energies that are getting rather than giving. That will rob you of your spiritual life. Think about this. If you are seeking to get as you pour forth these messages, getting will come back—as empty energy. As people seeking to get from you. Dear ones, the reverse of giving, which is Love, which is Christ, is then what we would name the anti-Christ.

This is why I am so fervently growing you. This is why I now speak to you of higher Will. This is why I ask you, dear ones, to be absolutely diligent in taking on the mantle of Christ, becoming the truth of your being. *Please study, think, and practice all that I have given in these*

Messages of Guidance to LightWorkers. Read them every day. Understand them enough to extract the precepts and place them in your heart.

I have told you how pure your intentions must be, how carefully chosen your inner landscape, how beautifully trained your mind, that your every thought is held in Love, vibrating the perfection of everything you look upon, thus awakening it. What you learn, dear ones, in the glorious ecstasy of your SoulMate unions will become who you are. You will embody the ecstasy that you access together. *Ultimately, dear ones, you will unfreeze this world of frozen Love just by gazing upon someone,* for your Consciousness (your mind), and your held Will will be joined, and everything you look upon, you will see its truth.

So to be a co-creator obviously does not mean using your smaller Will. Yet you cannot be immobilized, for truly, dear ones, it is only by living these truths that they become who you are. How then do you accomplish this? *By using gratitude to lift you into the vision of My Will for the person/circumstance you pray about and then bringing it into the world.* This can be done either by embodying the energies yourself or calling forth those who will.

Now I will begin to paint this picture in your consciousness, for you must have the whole picture. Then you will take all of the pieces into you and allow them to grow in you. Especially as you grow them with your SoulMate, they will be born into manifestation in your life swiftly. Then, beloved ones, you will all be the purest, most potent magnet for Christ manifesting in you and drawn into being around you. Perfectly, and then even more perfectly. Beloved ones, the hollow reed still knows its perfection as that reed. So will you know your perfection as Christ, for Christedness is the nature of your being. Knowing who you are, you will shape My Love as it pours through you. You will mold it in the shape of Christ. Thus will you blend your Will and Mine.

Now what on Earth does this mean? What does it mean now in your precious lives? What does it mean in your moments as you seek to clarify our inner landscape? It means that *praying gratitude with passion and energy will lift you up over any influence of the ego. As you pray gratitude in deep sincerity you are aligning yourselves with every Law of Love.* I am speaking here of the praying of gratitude that is passionately grateful for the perfection of each person and for every bit of good, every tiny bit, that they receive. This gratitude, dear ones, is first of all GIVING, for you are giving your Love and giving your blessings. You are giving your generous wishes for their highest good, and in doing so you are seeing that good. *This then is the perfect enactment of the process of co-creation.*

In this very process there is a fail-safe device. As you pray gratitude, dear ones, and do so genuinely, I will always come to lift you higher. I will always come, because essentially in doing such a process, you are "linking up." You are connecting yourselves right to the real electrical circuits of My heart. You may picture this as a cell of My heart coming alive. Beginning to flash! To light up. And first, of course, I am going to notice! Secondly, as you (this cell) get more and more charged, the sparks flying from you will eventually make contact with the nerve impulses or electricity of All I Am. In other words, you will then be "plugged in." Plugged in to Me and to all the energy that is life. Believe Me, dear ones, this changes everything. *So, dear ones, in the process of praying gratitude passionately without ceasing you are absolutely assured of doing My Will, not your little Will.*

As you pray gratitude, really pray it, you are lifted

up, you are connected, expanded, and in this state you will see My highest Will for whomever or whatever you are praying gratitude. It will simply be there in your consciousness. You will grasp in an instant the full picture of their highest good. It will be BIG. Bigger than you could have thought. It will be connected, for you are now connected to All That I Am. You will see all the ways these connections will work to lift and heal and benefit.

Then, dear ones, having received the vision of their truth, you will help to manifest it. You will come out of this passionate prayer of gratitude with the mold of their highest truth. This, dear ones, you will gently continue to hold it forth for them. You will bring it into the world. Using the sacred Womb of Creation, you, together as SoulMates, will bring it to birth. Thus, dear ones, will we co-create.

Now this will also work for creating for yourselves whatever you want for your life, dear ones. The difference is that by using this pattern you will be assured that your Will and My Will are one. You will start by praying gratitude as if the goal were already accomplished. Fervently. Passionately. You must not stop until you can feel yourselves being lifted up over the ego into the alignment with My Love. Then, in this union, you will see what My highest Will is for you in this area. Then you will set about manifesting it, bringing it into embodiment in the world. I can't stress enough how important this is. The coming of Christ is the Christ Consciousness coming to dwell in you, My beloved ones.

So you see, it is you who can and do choose the topic or the area to pray about. This is co-creating. But the difference is the next step. *You place it in the pattern of manifestation by thanking Me for its perfection while waiting on the revelation of My Will for this area/person/ situation/desire.* It is this, dear ones, that is the key. You will receive this vision, this experience of knowing the highest truth. This I promise you as long as you genuinely pray gratitude with your heart. Then you will see the perfection of Christ—the manifestation in perfect Love for that being/situation. In Love you will help bring that higher truth into the world, accomplished by your merging with Me through giving with your heart and thus receiving from Me the real truth of Love to be manifested.

I will continue to open this path wide for you as we travel the way of Love and the awakening of the mind and heart of Christ in and as SoulMates.

To The Reader

If you have resonated strongly with what you have just read, please know that there are in process at least two more books of Messages from God that continue the journey to Christ Consciousness. ***Say "Yes" to Love, God Leads Humanity Toward Christ Consciousness*** will be published within the next three to four months. If you would like to be kept informed of its publication date, please email us.

We also invite you to visit our Circle of Light website, www.circleoflight.net where Messages from God are posted on a variety of topics, as well as Questions and Answers, and Responses from readers. Features such as ***Read and Ponder*** highlight some of the most provocative and stimulating sections of very current Messages. You may also join our monthly email list for a monthly Message from God on different topics.

On the next few pages is an opportunity to ***Make a Personal Commitment to God***. Through the Messages, we have been assured that each person who follows the directions given will have a visible, tangible, personal experience of God.

We join our Love with your Love with the Love of brothers and sisters for the awakening of Love on our planet.

The Team at Circle of Light

YOU CAN HAVE A PERSONAL RELATIONSHIP WITH GOD

Make A Commitment To God Now.

God is preparing a Net of Living Love with which to lift the world, and is asking you to be a part. In recent Messages, God said "My Love is pursuing you. My grace now comes to stand before you, harder and harder to ignore–until beloveds, it will take more strength than all the legions of the lie to keep My grace from touching you and awakening you, My heart, into the Love you are."

God asks that you **make a written Commitment to open to God** (by whatever name is comfortable for you) **and begin a daily communion with God for yourself.** We have found that a wonderful time to do this is in the morning before getting out of bed, but it may be done at any time that fits your personal life schedule. The important thing is that it is done at least once daily and with consistency.

God has promised that each person who does this will have direct experience of a personal communion with God, "as long as they keep Hope alive and the Living Spirit connection in their life." It is each person's responsibility to keep the connection open. **"You will have all the light of Heaven coming to you."**

God has also asked that we at Circle of Light Spiritual Center act as a bridge, and each day bless and amplify every Commitment we receive, thus raising its vibration and magnifying the effect of its words. "...there will be those who begin to fly – whose hearts have wings – and they open to Me with great hunger and great joy. These we shall quickly add to the team of those who are part of the LightHouse."

God also has asked that each person make a list of the things for which they are grateful—"to include the success of their connection to Me, and a list of people to whom they wish to send My Love."

In Love, we deliver these instructions from the Messages from God as to how to proceed.

My Commitment To God

How To Proceed

Please fill out both Parts I and II below, and your name, address and email address. Keep a copy of what you have written for yourself to review several times daily. Mail or email a copy of your Commitment to us so that we may amplify it at Circle of Light Spiritual Center. If you wish, you may go to our website, www. circleoflight.net to post your Commitment.

As you begin to have experiences of God in your life, we would like to share them with others. If you feel comfortable, write out your experiences and send them to us. We will post them anonymously on the website for the inspiration and encouragement of others.

Part I

Please do use your own words but we give sample wording to assist you. You are of course not limited to what we suggest below. Be passionate; be real; speak your heart.

Write in the present tense, as though what you are doing has been already accomplished. Please KNOW that as you make this Commitment, you WILL begin to have direct experiences of God.

Sample wording: "I am making a deep commitment to open my heart and call God personally into my life each day. I am taking responsibility to maintain this connection, and I ask Circle of Light to amplify it for me in every way possible."

Part II

(a) Please write a list of things for which you are grateful, including the success of the above connection you are making with God. Again use the present tense. (b) Please also list people to whom you wish God to send Love.

MAIL OR EMAIL a copy of your Commitment to:

Circle of Light Spiritual Center
3969 Mundell Road
Eureka Springs, AR 72631
sayyes@circleoflight.net
www.circleoflight.net

ABOUT THE AUTHORS

Yaël and Doug Powell live at Circle of Light, a spiritual center in Eureka Springs, Arkansas, that looks out over Beaver Lake and the Ozark Mountains. Both Yaël and Doug are ordained ministers, and the lovely Chapel at Circle of Light is the frequent scene of beautiful sacred weddings.

Yaël spends a good deal of her time in bed as a result of pain from a severe physical disability. Her "up-time" is spent officiating at weddings or receiving the Messages from God in meditation. Doug is an artist and skilled craftsman at pottery and woodworking. If it is windy, you'll definitely find him at his lifelong passion–sailing! Shanna Mac Lean, compiler and editor of the Messages, also lives at Circle of Light. If not at the computer, she can be found in the organic vegetable garden.

Completing the Circle of Light family are their wonderful animal companions. Christos (boy) and Angel (girl) are their two beloved Pomeranians. Ariel (Duff Duff) is a pure white cat who mostly frequents the garden. Then there is Magic Cat, who has been with Yaël for 15 years. They have a deep and very special communion. Magic Cat has been communicating messages through Yaël to assist humans to understand the Web of Life. In the future, he will have his own book, "Magic Cat Explains God!"

CIRCLE OF LIGHT ORDER FORM
Say "Yes" to Love Series

Please send the following:

___ copies of *God Explains SoulMates* @ $11 ___ ($3 S&H)

___ copies of *God Unveils SoulMate Love & Sacred Sexuality* @ $19.95 ___ ($3.50 S&H)

___ copies of *God's Guidance to LightWorkers* @ $14 ___ ($3 S&H)

Prices are for the USA. For more than one book, reduce S&H on each book by $1. For postage to other countries, please email us first and we will find the best rate.

Name: _____

Address: _____

City: _____ State: ____ Zip Code: _____

To use credit cards, please go to our web site: www.circleoflight.net OR you may fax your order with credit card to (479) 253-2880. If it is busy, call 877-825-4448 and we will activate the fax.

Name on card: _____

CC#: _____ Exp date: _____

If you would like to be on our email list and receive monthly Messages from God, please fill out the following:

Email address: _____

Circle of Light
3969 Mundell Road
Eureka Springs, Arkansas 72631
www.circleoflight.net
Sayyes@circleoflight.net
1-866-629-9894 Toll Free
or 479-253-6832, 8132